Creativity, Inc.

Creativity, Inc.

Building an Inventive Organization

Jeff Mauzy
Richard Harriman

HARVARD BUSINESS SCHOOL PRESS

Boston, Massachusetts

Library of Congress Cataloging-in-Publication Data
Mauzy, Jeff.
    Creativity, Inc. : building an inventive organization / Jeff Mauzy, Richard
Harriman.
      p. cm.
    Includes index.
    ISBN 1-57851-207-7
    1. Creative ability in business. 2. Corporate culture. I. Harriman,
Richard A. II. Title.
HD53 .M375 2003
658.4'063—dc21

                                        2002154822

To Dan and Susanna,
my children just entering adulthood,
who have kept their creative sparks
despite any meddling on my part.
My wish is that they meet the
breadth and depth of their talents
as they keep on going.

—Jeff

To Ali, Michela, and Serena,
my daughters who help me see creativity
through their young eyes and who will be
the creators of the future.

—Rick

CONTENTS

Part Two

Climate

FOUR

The Climate for Creativity in an Enterprise
87

FIVE

Personal Creative Climate: The Bubble
103

Part Three

Action

SIX

Leadership: Fostering Systemic Creativity
117

SEVEN

Purposeful Creativity
145

EIGHT

Sustaining the Change
177

CREATIVITY, INC. has been written for people who share our conviction that it is important—in fact, essential in today's world—for organizations to nurture and apply creativity throughout their operations.

This premise ups the ante for many organizations, which in the past have relied on sporadic outbursts of creativity: the periodic product breakthrough, the isolated invention of a new service, the output of those in so-called creative departments. The need we see is for an enterprise to be creative at all times, in all areas, in all activities—what we call systemic creativity.

When systemic creativity is in place, creativity flourishes from top to bottom and across all functions. People and teams come up with blockbuster ideas that turn into multimillion-dollar products or even billion-dollar new businesses. Or they create ingenious marketing campaigns that ratchet up revenue, or lead process improvement programs that delight customers and employees alike, or implement restructuring initiatives that maximize cost reductions but minimize layoffs. And systemic creativity does not just apply to the big creative triumphs: People in organizations daily spark thousands of ideas that provide value in themselves and also build a higher plateau from which greater peaks of creativity can rise.

In other words, systemic creativity becomes an integral part of everyday operations and spawns the new thought, from small changes to breakthroughs, that organizations now need in every activity that makes a competitive difference.

For this to happen, creativity must become the responsibility of everyone—every leader and senior manager as well as every employee. Systemic creativity is only systemic when everyone in an organization learns how to practice it and then promotes it constantly.

Doing so is not easy. The behaviors required for successful creativity are out of tune with the behaviors that make a company operationally efficient, well-organized, and clear-sighted on its mission and goals.

There is no one "right" way to foster corporate creativity. There are, however, basic principles and practical techniques that have stood the test of time. We wrote this book to weave these principles and techniques into a workable framework and provide enough context, examples, and underlying theory to enable you to design and tailor approaches to the idiosyncrasies of your organization.

This book draws on our twenty-five years of experience in helping individuals, groups, and whole companies, from century-old Fortune 500 titans to new, venture-backed startups, to be more creative. It taps the knowledge of practitioners of corporate creativity, client and other, and creativity experts whose ideas have created their own breakthroughs in what remains a relatively nascent field.

Creativity, Inc. also capitalizes on the experiences of our colleagues past and present at Synectics Corporation, an international consulting firm widely recognized as a pioneer in the field of corporate creativity. Our founders' research on corporate creativity led to a seminal *Harvard Business Review* article, "An Operational Approach to Creativity," published in 1956.[1] Four years later they wrote a book, *Synectics,* and launched a consulting firm by the same name. In 1970, the firm published a book by Synectics cofounder George Prince, *The Practice of Creativity,* which was essential reading in the field for many years after its publication.[2]

Since 1960, Synectics has worked with organizations of nearly every stripe, from global manufacturers such as Kraft, Unilever, Pharmacia, and Coca-Cola, to service icons such as Citigroup, IBM, and Sainsbury. All in all, one out of every four companies on the Fortune 500 has brought in Synectics on assignments that demanded fresh solutions to issues such as replenishing dry new-product pipelines, rejuvenating lackluster marketing campaigns, developing whole new competitive strategies, and finding seemingly impossible ways to do more with less without wrecking corporate morale.

Many clients have said that these approaches made a profound difference by coaxing truly great ideas out of hiding and shepherding them over dangerous corporate terrain. These and other companies have taught us the most important lessons about what works and doesn't work in making organizations more creative and more competitive. *Creativity, Inc.* explores those lessons.

Jeff Mauzy
Richard Harriman
Cambridge, Massachusetts

ACKNOWLEDGMENTS

WE WOULD LIKE to express our deep gratitude to those who helped make this book a reality.

We extend affectionate thanks to George Prince, founder of Synectics and pioneer in the study of business creativity, who taught us the rudiments and with his passion fanned ours.

Teresa Amabile, David Perkins, and Jordan Peterson, leading psychologists and creativity researchers, willingly discussed portions of the book and provided great advice.

Margie Cigoy, Fred Faiks, Marty Mauzy, and Rachel Simmons reviewed drafts and offered valuable feedback that shows throughout.

We are greatly indebted to many people who were willing to share their experiences with us and in turn with the readers. Their thoughtfulness, passion, wisdom, and courage are lights to those who walk the path of discovery. Their names are listed at the end of this section.

A great deal of what we cover in this book has evolved from the continuous contributions about creativity approaches by our colleagues at Synectics. Thanks for the rich material, for the pleasure of working with you on challenging creativity assignments, and for your support during our time away from client work to pull this book together.

As facilitative consultants in creativity, we operate largely in the oral tradition in work that seldom follows straight lines. Translating this kind of talk into readable prose that tracks logically as a book has been a challenge. Katherine Andrews, Virginia LaPlante, and Nina Kruschwitz each in their own way helped shape the book, clear excess shrubbery, and bring coherence to the message. Thanks also to Siobhan Kelly and Teresa Blanchard for their administrative work and thoughtful contributions.

A very special thanks to Fred Dillen, whose aid and assistance in the writing of this book was invaluable.

Kristen Wainwright, we thank you for going beyond your role as literary agent and becoming an invaluable critic and editor.

For a number of reasons, among them the fact that we were not the fastest writers in the world, we had the pleasure of support from a number of people at the Harvard Business School Press—Janet Coleman, who initially suggested that we write the book, Marjorie Williams, Nikki Sabin, Jacqueline Murphy, and Jane Bonassar. Thank you all, with an extra note of appreciation to Jacque for her persistent faith and for her criticism, which was not only unerringly valuable but also delivered in a way that was easy to hear.

And last on this list but first in our thoughts, for our families who gave us time that would have been theirs on weekends and evenings and kept supporting us throughout, we express our appreciation, our debt, and our love.

Several of the people who offered their experiences and perspectives have moved from the companies with which they were affiliated when we interviewed them. Their known affiliations as of fall 2002 are listed.

Susan Adam, Publishers Clearing House; Eileen Ahlberg, Citigroup; Teresa Amabile, Harvard University; Maureen Arkle, Tufts Health Care Plan; Paul Barker, Hallmark Cards, Inc.; Jorge Bermudez, Citigroup; Lee Bloomquist, research consultant; Larry Bohn, Netgenesis, Inc.; Sam Borenstein, Citigroup; Darcy Bradbury, Mezzacappa Management, LLC; Lowry Burgess, Carnegie Mellon University; Jackie Burton, Citigroup; Peter Carlin, Jstreetdata, Inc.; Larry Cox, Raytheon, Inc.; Brian Crean, Guinness Ltd.; Matt Cutler, SPSS, Inc.; Barry Dayton, 3M Company; Elizabeth Deane, WGBH television; Nicholas Deane, Deane Redevelopment, Inc.; Paul Dietrich, Cambridge Seven Associates; Marylyn Dintenfass, artist; Bill Dunn, Baxter Healthcare Corporation; Terry Egger, St. Louis Post-Dispatch; Norm Elder, Universal Studios; Kaylee Engellener, Correctnet, Inc.; Fred Faiks, innovation consultant; Doug Farmer, retired; Marty Finegan, KPMG, Inc.; Lucien Frohling, banking consultant; Annie Gaudreault, Russell Branding, Inc.; John Gibson, Halliburton Company; Mark Greiner, Steelcase Inc.; William Hamlin, APL Ltd.; Gunter Henn, Henn Architekten GmbH; Rick Hensler, entertainment consultant; Phil Hettema, entertainment consultant; Lois Jacobs, Jack Morton Worldwide; Peter Jeff, Steelcase Inc.; Pete Karolczak, Hewlett-Packard Company; Rebekah Kaufman, communications consultant; Jon Kingsdale, Tufts Health Care Plan; Jim Keene, Steelcase Inc.; Hari Kulovaara, Royal Caribbean, Inc.; David Lathrop, Steelcase Inc.; Stephen Leichtman, Tufts Health Care Plan; Simon Lethbridge, Jack Morton Worldwide; Phillip Lindow, JP Morgan Chase & Company; Heiko Lotz, Deutsche Bank AG; Werner Low, communications consultant; Kathy Lundberg, Guidant, Inc.; Ron MacNeil, MIT; Deborah Marks, artist; Emerson Martlage, independent consultant; Dale Mason, Universal Studios; Jerry McAllister, 3M Company; Peter McGhee, WGBH television; Daniel McHugh, APL Ltd.; Rod McKay, KPMG, Inc.; Mary McKenney, banking consultant; Beverly Mehlhoff, Guidant, Inc.; Rick Mohr, Steelcase Inc.; Bob Miller, Correctnet, Inc.; Kurt Miller, Jack Morton Worldwide; Ray Miller, LSIL, Inc.; Geoff Nicholson, retired; Will Novosedlik, Taxi, Inc.; Conrad Paulus, Telcordia, Inc. (formerly AT&T Bell-Labs); Nic Pearce, independent consultant; Bob Peebler, Landmark Graphics, Inc.; David Perkins, Harvard University; Jordan Peterson, MIT; Carol Previte, Jack Morton Worldwide; Wayne Puglia, Nabisco Foods, Inc.; David Rabkin, Museum of Science,

Boston; Wendy Richmond, artist; Mary Ann Robbat, independent consultant; David Rose, Viant, Inc.; Bob Russell, Russell Branding, Inc.; Susan Sacks, Steelcase Inc.; Brian Shapard, Jack Morton Worldwide; Todd Sloan, Publishers Clearing House; Mary Sonnack, 3M Company; Eric Steidinger, Jack Morton Worldwide; Jack Tanis, Steelcase Inc.; Evelyn Tressitt, Deutsche Bank AG; John Wallingford, Wyeth, Inc.; David Welty, Hallmark Cards, Inc.; Laura Wills, Messenger, Inc.; Bill Wilson, retired; Pat Wnek, Graphic Packaging Corporation, Inc.; Mark Woodbury, Universal Studios.

Creativity, Inc.

Introduction

To survive and prosper in the long term, people in companies need to create and innovate. And they need to do so as regularly and reliably as they breathe.

We begin our discussion of the need for creativity with a look at a successful company that recognized and met a serious new challenge by installing effective creative practices. In the late 1980s, Steelcase Inc., one of the largest U.S. manufacturers of office furniture, like its competitors was investing heavily in research and development in the hot area of its business, modular furniture units.[1] "We had all evolved to the same perspective," says Mark Greiner, senior vice president of R&D at Steelcase. "There was an accepted framework in the industry, defined by three points on a triangle: high design, low cost, and customer relationship." Furniture companies had been differentiating themselves along the points of that triangle for some time. Steelcase was proudest of its customer relationships and placed most of its emphasis on maintaining that edge. "But in fact," Greiner says, "all the manufacturers, by watching each other, had gravitated over time toward safer and safer ground in the middle of the triangle defined by those three points." Thus, the differences between Steelcase and its rivals had grown almost nonexistent. "We were supposedly the most advanced office furniture company in the world, but in fact we were looking pretty much like our competition," he says.

Worse, the customer was in motion. The exciting technological liberties of computing and communications made office design and furniture seem less urgent, even less relevant to some businesses. This realization didn't come suddenly, says Greiner. "But it started creeping more often into our conversations. Where's the difference? What's our value?"

While the industry focused on a familiar, well-understood, highly defined world, the real world was changing. Steelcase needed to break free of many long-held beliefs about customer needs, beliefs that had become invalid. To reconnect with office furniture buyers, the company needed new ideas.

Steelcase in the late 1980s qualified as a candidate for creativity and innovation, and through the course of the book, we'll follow the Steelcase story.

But the Steelcase story is not unique. Corporate leaders in almost any business today need to know the fundamental elements for initiating and sustaining creativity and innovation. And they must understand the ways in which those elements work together.

The speed of change in the economy has long since penalized companies and industries that try to coast with scattershot innovation or a single moment of creative serendipity. It now punishes even strategically astute companies that make serious but only sporadic, isolated, or conventional efforts at creativity and innovation.

In the 1870s, Aaron Ward targeted quality-and-value-starved rural shoppers with a single-page, cash-only price list mailed to National Grange members. There was enough creativity and innovation in that business plan to start Montgomery Ward on a 125-year run. The only further innovation of any scope, however, was to build out stores across the country, a strategy that within a few decades caused the company to fall so far behind the pace of change in contemporary imagination and desires that customers stayed away.[2]

Still, 125 years is a good ride. Increasingly, the time period that an innovation can last is far shorter. Look at the home audio music business. The music box controlled that market for 100 years. The phonograph controlled the market for 70 years. Cassette tapes dominated for 25 years until the arrival of CDs. Now, after 10 years, CDs compete with mini-disks, DVDs, MP3, and the Internet.

And, as if the inexorable compounding in the rate of technological change weren't sufficiently uncomfortable, consider Digital Equipment Corporation and Wang. In 1985, the two pioneering computer companies were at the top of their business and successfully defending their competitive advantages by locking in corporate customers with exclusive networks of proprietary machinery and software. Within a decade both companies were as good as gone, victims of a home computing and open architecture evolution that bypassed their proprietary protections.

Not only, then, does competitive advantage have a time limit, a limit shrinking before the accelerating pace of technological change, but resources given to protecting today's competitive advantage can distract companies from keeping an eye on the creative work of developing and deploying the innovations that could drive tomorrow's business.

Harvard Business School professor Rosabeth Moss Kanter draws an analogy between doing business now and playing croquet beside Alice in Wonderland, with the mallets, balls, wickets, and stakes all alive and all whimsically free to decide when and how they want to move.[3] And Dartmouth business professor Richard D'Aveni says that relying too long on a competitive advantage is like "shoveling sand against the tide."[4]

The message in all this, as Steelcase found out, is that tomorrow, with all its surprises, comes more relentlessly and more quickly than ever before. To respond to and take advantage of the surprises, individuals and companies will want to be as ready as possible. And readiness requires creativity.

We contend that the successful companies will have established constant, systemic creativity. They'll do so to fuel the moment-to-moment innovative responses a high-speed marketplace demands. They'll do so to maintain imaginative resources that can project operations into a future that will change even faster than the present. They'll do so to develop, in our here-and-gone business environment, the reliably pliable foundations from which breakthrough innovations can be launched.

Companies will strive to become systemically creative because creativity pays. It pays financially and it provides a rich array of other rewards: employee and customer satisfaction, incremental growth, the flexibility to match relentless change, the ability to attract good talent, elevated market interest, and strengthened competitive readiness. The rewards of some of the creativity programs that we explore in the book are illustrative:

- Early into a creativity change program, APL/NOL, a major ocean shipping company, has measured an impact of $46.6 million from cost reduction and avoidance, revenue increase, and improved asset management.

- Tufts Health Care, now the second-largest HMO in New England, reached its goal of one million members two years ahead of schedule, tripling its membership in five years. Since then it has launched eleven significant new products or services and won four innovation awards. In 1999 *Newsweek* ranked THCP second among U.S. managed care plans across all categories surveyed. And CareData, the health-care division of J.D. Power, has rated THCP the best overall HMO in metropolitan Boston every year since 1996.

- Snack-food giant Frito-Lay attributed more than $100 million in cost reductions to creativity training sessions for employees.

- Medical equipment maker Guidant leaped onto *Fortune*'s list of the top 100 companies to work for, coming in thirty-first in its first try.
- The diversified technology company 3M, aggressively pursuing innovation, estimates that it has generated more than $4 billion from new product introductions for each of the last four years.
- People under the leadership and creativity support of Peter McGhee, vice president of national programming at WGBH, a public broadcasting company in Boston, have earned it more than fifty Emmy awards, thirty-seven Peabody awards for broadcast excellence, and twenty-five duPont-Columbia journalism awards.
- Sysco Corporation, a $23 billion food distributor, reports that employees who participated in creativity training increased their sales an average 25 percent to 30 percent.
- With the addition of Islands of Adventure, attendance at Universal Studios' two Florida theme parks climbed 11 percent between 2000 and 2001, while crowds at Disney's four Florida parks dropped 6 percent.
- In its first year, Steelcase's Leap chair, born from the company's new direction and magnified focus on the user, became one of the top-selling chairs in the world.

In *Creativity, Inc.,* our goal is to enhance a company's ability to create and innovate—reliably, systemically, without stop. We start with six essential understandings that weave through the book and the creative process.

There is no recipe for systemic creativity. There is no fixed recipe for all or even most companies. The field of systemic creativity and innovation is still so immature that there are none of the requisite benchmarks needed for universal recipes. In fact, our experience suggests that while more specific guidelines will evolve, a more complete and replicable formula for creative success will be elusive for quite some time. So, instead of a recipe, *Creativity, Inc.* provides the foundational principles and practices a company needs to build the framework that's right for itself.

Creativity and innovation are two distinct concepts. Although people often use the terms interchangeably, creativity and innovation differ from one another. Each demands different treatment, and each has a different science. To paraphrase Harvard Business School's Teresa Amabile, a leading researcher in the field, creativity is the generation of novel and appropriate ideas.[5] Innovation, as we define it, implements those ideas and thereby changes the order of things in the world.[6]

Creativity is about breaking down prior assumptions and making new connections for new ideas. Innovation means taking new ideas and turning them into corporate and marketplace reality. True innovation, as opposed to low-level refinement, takes extended creative effort, yet much of the innovation effort lends itself to direction and organizing. It's much harder to organize, direct, and command the creation of first ideas; you have to encourage and tease out creativity individual by individual. Both creativity and innovation need to be nurtured at every level and function for a corporation to become systemically creative.

Creativity happens with individuals, coalitions and teams, and organizations. Systemic creativity, sustained creativity throughout a company, has three operating arenas: individual creativity, the creativity practiced by coalitions and teams, and the support that organizations give to each. Once individuals have a clear sense of their own creativity wellspring, they can revitalize creativity in themselves and in the people around them. Creativity for coalitions and teams begins with the fragile process of moving from creativity to innovation. Finally, for success, a company needs to prepare itself to provide the resources, the strategy, and the climate that encourage both individuals and groups to perform at their creative best. Only with the grasp of and the practice in all three of these arenas is it possible to think and operate creatively on a full corporate scale.

There are four critical dynamics. Underlying creativity are four linked, interacting dynamics: motivation, curiosity and fear, the breaking and making of connections, and evaluation. Fluency in these dynamics will guide individuals and companies in reclaiming, using, and polishing creativity and innovation. Ultimately, these four dynamics are the heartbeat of systemic creativity.

Creativity depends on climate. Climate has an overwhelming influence on the success of creativity. Creativity does not occur in a vacuum; it needs a sympathetic environment. Individuals need to build a climate to nourish and protect their own creativity from the indifference or hostility of the larger climate. Companies need to transform the larger climate into one that actively supports creativity throughout the organization.

Systemic creativity asks everyone to be a leader. Each person in a company has the potential for leadership in creativity. With systemic creativity, there are no artificial designations between "creative" people and "everyone else." Everyone can be creative. Everyone is responsible for sparking ideas and shepherding them into useful innovation. A receptionist, no less than a corporate manager, can observe an unhappy customer, create an idea to correct the situation, and work to make the idea happen. Anyone who takes this initiative leads.

Creativity, Inc. divides the exploration of its themes into three parts: Part I, Creative Thinking; part II, Climate; and part III, Action. The first six chapters, parts I and II, cover building capability for creative thought. The final three chapters, part III, put creativity to purposeful work.

Part I, Creative Thinking, addresses the dynamics of personal, team, and corporate creativity. How does individual creativity work, what gets in the way of it, and how can one reinvigorate it? And group creativity—how does creativity work on an enterprise scale, so that everyone in the organization can give his or her creative best and boost company performance?

Part II, Climate, discusses creativity and its environment. The degree to which people and companies benefit from creativity depends on the degree to which a company provides a climate sympathetic to the dynamics of the creative process. This section discusses creative climates and how to nourish them for individuals and for companies.

Part III, Action, presents a guide and examples for purposeful, focused innovation. It explores the demands and possibilities of business leaders who aspire to systemic creativity and discusses the constant call to sustain and reinvent creative initiative.

Part One

Creative Thinking

ONE

The Dynamics That Underlie Creative Thinking

ONE CAN BE CREATIVE without understanding the underlying dynamics much as one can drive a car without understanding how the engine works. In fact, as consultants, we often facilitate creative sessions in which we devote little time to covering the underlying dynamics with people who are responsible for generating new ideas.

Our knowledge allows us to introduce exercises that participants can work with to get successful results. However, for the purposes of assisting readers who want to promote greater creativity within their company, we believe some basic understanding is an invaluable foundation.

The creative process is a cerebral one, and the study of the brain in relation to creativity, much like the study of corporate creativity, is young. Theories in both fields continue to evolve and overlap. We monitor development in both fields, and, along with our colleagues, we continuously experiment to ascertain whether and how a new perspective might be translated into an effective practical tool. Through this practice, and rubbing up against new research, we have identified four dynamics that we believe are important to understand: motivation, curiosity and fear, breaking and making connections, and evaluation. These dynamics are the foundation of the creative process. They are collectively the touchstone to which individuals and companies can return to re-energize perspective when creativity slips out of reach. They are the basic dynamics individuals and companies engage in when stimulating and sustaining creativity.

Before tackling the dynamics, let's clear the air of some misconceptions about creativity. First, creativity is not reserved for artists, inventors, creative professionals, and the handful of visionaries who in other venues change the way everyone understands their lives. True, these folks work far more frequently and intensely with the creative dynamics than the rest of the population. They get practice in the creative process, and so they become adept at it.

But many more people don't credit themselves with the artistry of the meals they cook, the jokes they tell, or even the inventiveness behind a creative commute. Neither does the world take much notice of that sort of creativity. And usually, such moments of artistry and invention occupy only a small part of anybody's time. In fact, most people don't get a lot of practice at creativity; they don't expect much of it when they do practice it, and so their creativity atrophies.

But we have found, and science agrees, that everyone, artist or not, is capable of being creative. Divergent thinking, the ability to make mental connections between unrelated matters, is one commonly accepted indicator of creative capacity. Studies show that 98 percent of children aged three to five score near the top of the scale on divergent thinking, while only 2 percent of adults over the age of twenty-five have comparable scores.[1] Furthermore, individuals who have lower scores at age five and remain creatively active may easily outperform others who initially score higher but do not exercise their creativity.

Society, acculturation, and formal education wean most people so completely from creative exercise that if they ever venture into creative competition, they don't survive any better than couch potatoes thrown into a decathlon. But that doesn't have to be the case. Everyone is born with innate creative ability, and creative ability responds to exercise like a muscle. And although not everyone may be a natural Olympian of creativity, anyone who gets into shape can surely run and jump and bounce the ball.

How do you get into shape for creativity? You learn how creativity works, and you practice it. In the pages ahead, we outline the basics and help you begin exercising.

Motivation

Psychologist Jordan Peterson describes motivation as a function of the difference between what people expect to happen if they don't intervene and what they desire. In this sense, motivation is the measure of the emotional investment it takes for people to break natural inertia, to move away from their attachment to their current circumstances and to move toward what they want.[2] As a simplistic example, most young adults at some point find themselves without, say, wealth or romantic love. If they want either or both and want them enough to do something about it, they have motivation. The distance between circumstances and desire creates emotional pressure that activates somebody to do something new—to get a job, to put on clean clothes and look for a date. This activating desire, motivation, is the dynamic that starts a person into the creative process.

People often live amid a fluctuating multitude of motivations because they want so many different things at the same time. The psychologist Fritz Perls says, "In reality life is one unfinished state followed by others, often not allowing for any closure before new challenges emerge."[3]

Heiko Lotz, a director involved in strategic business development at Deutsche Bank, works to keep his bank on a stable course into whatever circumstances the future holds. The likely gap between a high-speed, unpredictable future and a desired future of stability is clear and wide. But for Lotz, "change is the biggest opportunity you can imagine," and closing the gap between disparate and changeable futures provides motivation that he relishes.[4]

Lotz's job is to understand present and future competition and create initiatives that will keep his bank competitive. He looks at what both traditional and nontraditional companies are doing. He uses the information he gathers to construct scenarios of competitive environments in which the bank may find itself three to five years out. Then he analyzes the scenarios in terms of his bank's product portfolio, investment decisions, client base, and strategic planning. "We not only have to identify the right strategic initiatives to pursue based on those scenarios, we have to be able to create new plans quickly, continually recreating a bank that can prosper in them." His thinking must include designing broad market entry strategies and specific business plans for geographical regions and target clients. He must come up with potential strategic alliances, joint ventures, acquisitions, and divestitures. As Lotz explains, alternate future scenarios multiply the possibilities of all of these actions. Each needs its own plan. Energized by the difference between the vision of a stable bank in the future and the likelihood that the future business environment will be anything but stable, Lotz creates his scenarios to discover a stable course for the bank no matter what happens.

Lotz's paycheck is not his primary motivator. The work suits him. He naturally embraces change. His motivation is a prime example of what psychologist Abraham Maslow calls the self-actualization growth instinct, one of the most satisfying motivations of mankind.[5]

Motivation in Creativity Companywide

In the introduction, we discussed Steelcase, which had a sound, traditional R&D program and then found that its R&D

efforts needed to change to meet the user needs its research was uncovering. Steelcase was in the furniture business and wanted to stay in the furniture business, yet the customer had moved. Though the company was entrepreneurial for a furniture manufacturer, it was ill-prepared to move with the speed of computer and communications start-ups.

Steelcase was a solid company, but it needed to quickly change to keep pace with the speed of changing customer needs. That's motivation of a different sort than the self-actualization sought by Heiko Lotz. The company was no less motivated than Lotz, but it was motivated by the basic need to survive—change or die. Steelcase was at the other end of Maslow's hierarchy of needs.

Extrinsic and Intrinsic Motivation

Harvard professor Teresa Amabile, drawing from her research in creativity, describes two sources of motivation, extrinsic and intrinsic.[6] Extrinsic motivation is a reaction to—is driven by—external rewards such as money and fame. While powerful in stimulating various kind of actions, extrinsic motivation tends to diminish the quality of creativity, unless, as Amabile found, it occurs in a specific and right relationship to intrinsic motivation. In certain of these right relationships between extrinsic and intrinsic motivation, where extrinsic motivation serves a high intrinsic motivation, Amabile found that creative quality could be slightly increased.[7] Intrinsic motivation comes from a person's or company's natural affinity. It is associated with passion and even fun and also with high creative quality. Heiko Lotz, in aiming for self-actualization through embracing change, is intrinsically motivated.

Kurt Miller, creative director at Jack Morton Worldwide, an international communications firm, illustrates a combined set of intrinsic and extrinsic motivation. The extrinsic motivation, driven by salary and deadline, is to help clients communicate their business to their target audience. A lot of effort goes into distilling the message to the client's audience and then identifying the vehicle of common experience in which to deliver that message.

Miller finds his intrinsic motivation within the workings of salary-driven client service.

> *We often use a metaphor or mental construct to concentrate the message. This is when I get to play. Lately, for example, I've been fascinated by James Dean, the actor known for playing a rebel in the fifties. He had the ability to say, "Go to hell" and "Help me" simultaneously. I'm frequently looking for an opportunity to express the same kind of contradictory feeling or double message, and integrating it into the essence of my client's message.*[8]

Merging the extrinsic demands for a timely client solution with his own intrinsic interest benefits everyone. "As an artist, I need to express myself even though I'm working for someone else. There would be no spark, no personality, without my subjective . . . need coming into my work. When I'm doing my best, I'm satisfying both goals."

The importance of intrinsic motivation also shows up in more traditional business functions. A colleague of Miller's at Jack Morton sells the company's creative services to about eighty clients. The clients she spends the most time on are those she finds have "an interest that touches me." She has a higher level of happiness and satisfaction when working with these clients and, not surprisingly, better relationships with them. And it's on the projects for these clients, Miller says, "where we usually do our best work."

Jack Morton Worldwide is competing for the dollars of clients, and the employees are striving to advance in their jobs—all extrinsic motivators. But real success, the best, most creative work, comes when interior, intrinsic motivation is engaged alongside the extrinsic.

To begin the creativity process, every individual and every company needs motivation. In corporate cultures built entirely on traditionally extrinsic motivations, creativity will be seen as a distraction from the historically proven straight line to earnings and power. The more intrinsic the motivation, the better the creative result.

Curiosity and Fear

The process of creativity begins at any point, but in the usual and most natural cycle, once you are motivated, your curiosity follows. Along with it, all too frequently, comes fear.

Curiosity

If you're motivated strongly enough to defeat your current circumstances, then you are moved to action, and the next step is to begin the search for possibly useful information. This search is curiosity, the psychic state whereby people explore the unknown possibilities that motivation makes manifest.[9] Curiosity is an aspect of the search for knowledge and sense. It leads people to experiment with their environment; it leads them to unplanned discoveries. As we'll discuss shortly, these discoveries, and particularly the journeys through the unknown that lead to them, are often fearful. They are also often surprisingly playful. In both cases, they give people experience on which to draw for understanding new circumstances.

Curiosity, when exercised in safe experimentation, transforms the unknown from something potentially dangerous into something manageable, perhaps interesting, even beneficial.[10] Think about Heiko Lotz in this context. He's trying to bridge the gap between the stability of his bank and the change that the future promises. He's motivated by change, excited by the opportunities it presents, and this motivation ignites his curiosity about the future, what will happen, what the changes will be. He searches with avid curiosity for clues about future circumstances for the bank and, with the clues, he creates a scenario laying out another possibly stable course in the unknown future.

Or consider an executive in a manufacturing company that historically sold just equipment. Predictions of the future of the equipment industry made it clear to him that he wouldn't achieve his dream of doubling his company's earnings in five years unless he found a new path. Among his options, he and the guiding coalition he formed focused on redefining the company's business to provide complete solutions of which equipment would be only a part—and in terms of profits, an ever smaller part.

This would be a significant change for the company in many ways, and the team wondered how to proceed. There were no models for a transition from product provider to solutions provider in their industry. And in other areas, such as the defense and computer industries, where there had been somewhat analogous transitions, the situations were in fact much too different for best-practices benchmarking. Motivated by a general exploratory curiosity, he arranged for the team to consult with people from the defense and computer industries simply to find out what the key elements were in their transition efforts and what they thought they ought to consider.

Their companies had suffered great pain and had needed considerable change, and the people from the companies felt that the pain had provided the stimulus for successful change. There was very little felt pain at the equipment manufacturer, however, as business was still strong—it was the future that presented a problem. So the defense and computer people advised the equipment executive to consider waiting until the company experienced enough pain to sustain the high level of change required in any transition to solutions provider.

The equipment executive did not take this advice, but it sent his curiosity into a new area. He wondered now about how to feel and draw stimulation from pain that was inevitable but that had not yet arrived. And he continued to wonder about how the company would best respond to that stimulation. This evolving curiosity led to a realization that flexible, reoriented, and re-freshed leadership might be the company's great need as it anticipated pain and change. Accordingly, he helped lead a powerful new leadership development program that would give the company the skills it needed for whatever path it had to follow in the transition to solutions provider.

Curiosity and New Insight

Often people who are motivated and curious and who break loose of inhibitions reach into new experiences and uncover knowledge that is beyond the sensible, anticipatory scenario building that Lotz practices.

Mary Ann Robbat, a new director at a young Internet company, was designing an interactive computer program to help employees of a client company assess their competence for advancement in the company. The design was tricky. The program asked for a lot of personal information. If employees disclosed the information only to discover that they needed many more skills to advance in their careers, they might be discouraged from ever using the program again—which would prevent them from capturing the very real service the program could provide them and their company.

One day on a recreational trip to New York, Robbat saw and was transfixed by a Mark Rothko painting.[11] As she says, "I stood in front of his painting and felt I could just walk into it, into the large squares of inviting simple color, into a warm and open world beyond." She knew that the experience held an insight for her, and she stood looking at the Rothko painting for some time.

Back at the office, thinking about her program, the idea came to her. If color could convey hospitality and security and openness so powerfully in a painting, it could speak to other people the same way in other media. A warm, sympathetic palette of colors carrying the program onto an employee's computer screen could create the feeling of welcome and trust that would make personal disclosure seem less risky and might minimize initial frustration.

Robbat became sure that the right colors could solve the program's problem. And she was right. The color, painstakingly determined, actually did promote and maintain employee engagement with the software program. Robbat's curiosity, opened to encompassing unexpected experiences by a problem that absorbed her, searched her own response to a painting and found just the necessary insight.

Fear

As someone searches curiously through new experience for unimagined knowledge, they reach into the unknown. And that, like reaching barehanded through the dark, is often frightening. For some of us, a little bit of fright can change to powerful fear. And unmanaged, fear can escalate to the point where it triggers a primitive "fight-or-flight" response that focuses thinking and behavior purely on survival.[12] If sufficiently frightened, we lose most capacity for creative curiosity. So it is that employees faced with new but potentially risky tasks avoid beginning them. Similarly, the creative output of entire companies slows down during layoffs.[13]

Here's a conundrum that comes into play with individuals and with companies. Curiosity engages the unknown. Curiosity increases uncertainty and an attendant element of fear. In moments of fear, curiosity becomes hard to sustain. And yet without curiosity's advance into the sometimes fearful unknown, people avoid the new experience from which they might gain insight. Jordan Peterson says that learning is necessarily "a creative encounter with the unknown."[14]

Educational researchers Peter Okebukola, Kinnard White, and Gerald Matthews have all shown that "an experience of dread and foreboding" correlates poorly with creativity.[15] And yet curiosity and creativity do often thrive despite fear. Guilty, exposed, and rightly nervous children occasionally summon the wherewithal to talk their furious parents out of punishment. Anxious Ph.D. candidates manage to defend their theses.[16] At one level, most people learn by exposure to life to manage their fears and increase their tolerance for risk. The employee who once avoided tackling new projects because he feared mistakes or failure can learn to remind himself of past successes, to move on after the occasional failure, and to communicate with his boss about appropriate expectations.

At a deeper level, each person has a different tolerance for risk. To some extent risk tolerance is determined by the motivation involved. Intrinsically motivated people are able to tolerate greater risk and more fear. Think about Heiko Lotz. For some people, the responsibility of preparing a sizable bank for life or death in endless and imminent variations of the perilous future would bring on ulcers. For Lotz, interest in change is a natural gravitation. And keep in mind that Lotz envisions scenarios facing his bank five and ten years out; the risk is so far in the future that fear does not constrict his curiosity and creativity in the present moment.

As Peterson might observe, Lotz is managing his fear and curiosity in a balance that allows him to remain creative now. When someone anticipates fear and exercises curiosity well in advance of the point at which the fear would become intolerable, the person can make the fear manageable enough to either discount it or turn it to productive use.

Peter McGhee, vice president for national programming at WGBH, says that in his business, "the fear of failure can be overwhelming. One young producer was so crushed by negative reviews of her work that she was unable to take up her next project."[17]

The solution, according to McGhee, lies in such strong intrinsic belief in the work that you can commit yourself beyond the point of possible discouragement. "You have to fall passionately in love with your project and allow yourself to become obsessed." McGhee acknowledges fear, but he puts sufficient stock in his intrinsic motivation and interest to move through the fear with creative curiosity intact.

Sometimes, there's no choice but to seize on the discomfort of counterbalancing risks and safety in a tough situation. Athletes do this in competition where the consequences of not being curious, of not trying a higher degree of dive and losing to the competition, become greater than the fear of failing at the dive. The ability to confront risks head on without freezing up or defaulting to the acceptance of loss often separates the winning athletes from the losing athletes.

Breaking and Making Connections:
Forming New Ideas

Breaking and making connections is where most of the work of creativity gets done. Picasso said, "The creative act is first and foremost an act of destruction." We say he was talking about connection breaking.[18] By destruction, we do not mean destruction of a company but rather destruction of rigid sets of assumptions about what can and can't be done in a particular marketplace. Business assumptions can be an efficient shortcut to making consistent decisions, but in the context of creativity, assumptions inhibit the making of vital new connections.

For example, conventional wisdom assumed that books needed to be sold primarily through bookstores. This assumption was broken at least twice, and in both instances the break stimulated profitably creative connections. The first break with the bookstore assumption led to the idea of sales in airports, convenience stores, and supermarkets. A second break led Amazon.com to Internet sales.

We argue that breaking and making connections is where the fundamental action of the creative process takes place, and what's known in the fields of psychology and brain physiology lines up with this. For the following material about the brain, we draw broadly on the work of a number of researchers and theorists.[19]

Connections in the Networked Mind

The brain contains from a hundred billion to a trillion neurons, and each neuron connects by synapses to anywhere from one hundred to ten thousand other neurons. Memory resides not in a specific location but in the order and timing of this neural excitation.

Once a stimulus produces a particular sequence of neural firings, each cell nucleus manufactures proteins that attach along that signal's pathway. When repetition of the same stimulus causes repetition of the same neural firings, more proteins are manufactured and attached to reinforce the signal pathway. The more the signal goes out, the more its pathway is reinforced. And the more the pathway is reinforced, the more easily it's recalled.

As people repeat these cerebral experiences, they are essentially forming patterns of remembered association between connections. To the extent the patterns continue to successfully align with the world that people perceive, people continue to use and reinforce them, and they come to trust them. With sufficient use and trust, the patterns establish themselves as knowledge and as the basis for new patterns of extended knowledge.

People apply their most reinforced patterns of connection—their knowledge—to the challenges and possibilities of the world around them. People decide what to do based on their patterns of connection. Taken to the extreme, these protein-reinforced patterns can become the associative ruts that people get into. People function most creatively when they break out of their reinforced patterns to establish new connections between disparate patterns, thus shaping new configurations of the neural pathways in response to new challenges and possibilities. There's nothing exotic in this; it happens every day, though it does happen many more times a day during childhood, when people are learning at a faster pace.

For a child, everything is new and all of it is a river of constant, natural breaking and making of connections. A child's first, most frequent associations with "cup" might have to do with holding water, and those associations might, through the synapses of day-to-day experience, naturally include other types of liquid and other sorts of vessels. Those day-to-day synapses, the ordinary growth of understanding (a jar can hold orange juice) represent creative breaks with previous, fixed patterns and establishment of new connections, new patterns, cup to jar, water to orange juice.

Connections: Creating with Stored Information

Most day-to-day creativity occurs when, over time, people have gained large amounts of interconnected knowledge in select areas. A sales director comes to know her company's products, markets, and customers, and the skills necessary to manage her operations. Her amassed knowledge helps her to make broader and faster inferences when negotiating and to more easily supply solutions when problems arise. Her knowledge also gives her a storehouse of relevant material with which to work when she needs a wholly new solution.

The chef Julia Child acquired such broad experience with French foods and cooking techniques that she routinely created new recipes. Thomas Edison's background in early electrical engineering made it likely that his creativity would lead to electrical inventions. Similarly, in finding new solutions, the sales director has to break free of entrenched connections, or assumptions, that don't work in whatever new circumstance may arise. Once she makes the break, she's immersed in such a wealth of new and handy connections that she's likely to come up with the appropriate new configuration of patterns easily.

A motivated, curious mind, practiced in connection breaking, can escape inhibiting assumptions and make the subsequent connection to new ideas in any domain. A dearth of raw material for relevant connections, however, will lessen the frequency of ideas and will also make it hard to recognize and evaluate the ideas that are truly new and useful.

Connecting Between Disciplines

Although people are more creatively prolific in their particular discipline, this very expertise is often a hindrance to discovery. Looking to patterns of information from entirely different disciplines helps break up current lines of thinking and old assumptions. It is a useful way to start new connections.

In 1998, Larry Cox, a scientist at MIT's Lincoln Laboratory, was looking for a noninvasive method to monitor glucose in the human body. At the time, diabetics had to test their insulin level four or more times a day by pricking a finger to draw blood. This procedure was painful, prone to infection, and left pin tracks all over the diabetic's fingers. Cox wanted a test that avoided breaking the skin.

As he worked on the problem, brainstorming with colleagues in his field, Cox's curiosity antennae were up and searching for more potential links. The breakthrough came when he talked with a scientist working outside his field. The other scientist had recently experimented with electroporation, a procedure that allowed medicine to be administered without breaking the skin by applying an electrical charge to the skin, which widened the pores.

There it was. "I realized we don't need to porate the skin completely." Cox had made the creative mental break; he didn't necessarily have to avoid going through the skin to avoid the invasive pinpricks. "We just needed to make the glucose more accessible to the surface of the body by opening pores underneath the surface layer and bringing blood closer to our instruments, which were sensitive enough to measure it."[20] And with his break with the medical assumptions about his problem, Cox could then make the connection between two seemingly unrelated approaches in two quite distinct disciplines.

It's also in the interdisciplinary arena that Steelcase played out the next chapter in its story. Motivated by the desire to differentiate its product, Steelcase began to think differently about the frameworks of understanding on which it based its product decisions. "Ten or so years ago there was a concept team that went out to New Mexico, near Albuquerque, to think," explains Mark Greiner, senior vice president of R&D. "We asked ourselves what the next generation of office was going to be like." Out of that work, the conceptual thinkers at Steelcase developed the notion of what they called Pathways. Pathways articulates the flow of utilities and capabilities, such as power, voice, and LAN cables, through a building's architecture. Pathways is something like the umbilical cord of an office, and at Steelcase, people started to consider how those pathways defined the use of, and the need for, furniture. And there: That was a basic assumption, a profound connection, broken—Steelcase had always previously understood pieces of furniture to be objects in space but not integral to the space. Then here, following the connection broken, came the new connection made: Furniture had to plug into the pathways of an office; office furniture needed to be interdependent with the critical office pathways. If it wanted to prosper and grow, Steelcase needed to, and now saw the opportunity to, work with clients to structure and furnish comprehensive, uniquely adapted business environments aligned with the flow of technology. Steelcase broke out of purely traditional furniture manufacturing and made the connection into a large, new, and distinct discipline, a discipline that, as we'll see in chapter 3, demanded plenty of creativity in its own right.

Extraordinarily useful connections are there to be made if companies or individuals can bring themselves to break the old connections to patterns that no longer work.

Messy Connections

Finding meaningful new connections involves sorting through many possibilities, most of which appear to have little relevance. In our work, seemingly irrelevant connections often turn out to have profound relevance. That Mark Rothko's painting inspired a solution to Mary Ann Robbat's Web site problem is a case in point. Robbat's curiosity made her receptive to her surprising response to the color in a painting, which led her to imagine color as a solution to her problem.

Is there breaking and making of connections in the path from Robatt's curiosity sparking on a color to her final solution? There is, and at a couple of different stages. First, Robatt says, "I wouldn't have believed you could walk through a color until his work showed me." Her apparently unfocused curiosity produced an idea that broke down her conceptions about color and physical boundaries. Then that idea allowed a more applied curiosity at the office to break down the assumptions about the barriers between painting and software, and that in turn helped make the connection between the use of color and the sympathetic engagement of the audience for her program.

Exercising curiosity is not always easy, and, as Robatt discovered, it can be confusing to pursue the new connections that curiosity sometimes uncovers. Sometimes, good creative connections even seem contradictory.

Elizabeth Deane, an executive producer for public television, had come of age when Richard Nixon's presidency was ending in disgrace. She held a low opinion of Nixon, and that lack of regard had been reinforced by the cultural perception of the time. "I wasn't a knee-jerk Nixon-hater," Deane says, "but I knew him mainly in the context of Vietnam and Watergate, and I didn't see much to admire or respect in the man." Then one day Deane read that Nixon was credited with orchestrating the triumph of the first SALT treaty, a treaty widely regarded as a high moral good. The article mentioned that the Watergate break-in, the catalyst for Nixon's disgrace, took place only a few days after the signing of that SALT treaty.

> *I was in my office, looking outside, sort of hovering over this information, when things in my mind suddenly got very quiet. For me, those two events, so starkly different in nature, and so close together in time, really captured a complexity that made Nixon much more interesting, both as a president and as a man. I could see that you have to accept those conflicts and ambiguities in order to understand him. I knew then that I wanted to do a film about this man.*[21]

For Deane to see Nixon as anything but unequivocally flawed was a major break with a long-established assumption. To recognize his complexity, to understand him as human, was a remarkable new connection. Not only did she break old connections that until that hour had seemed articles of faith, she made new ones that an hour before would have seemed absurd. Often, when incompatible sets of information collide, we can ignore the new data in favor of old knowledge, replace old knowledge with the new, or find a third resolution, which Deane did when she, to her surprise, rediscovered Nixon as a deeply flawed person containing redemptive virtue, a person worthy of explication. "He's not a tragic hero, but there is something tragic about him," Deane says of the Nixon who emerged in her film.

Evaluation

Evaluation is the last dynamic in the foundation of the creative process. Because choices are seldom cut and dried, fruitful evaluation is a balancing act. Is this better than that, and if so, is it enough better to justify quitting the search for the ideal? Should some parts of a new but flawed concept be saved for use in a later, as yet unknown, answer? If an evaluation proves altogether negative, does it make sense to recharge motivation and curiosity, to begin new cycles of breaking and making connections? Or not? Given an encouraging evaluation, will the new solution that looks good now hold up for long, and how long is long enough?

It takes time and energy to consider all possibilities among or within competing concepts. Resistance to undertaking any one concept can be enormous. Reverberations from the public humiliation of failure can end careers that have even slight association with the creative attempt. So if a flaw shows up in a corporate idea, there's a powerful temptation to drop it after a quick evaluation and perhaps abort the whole creative endeavor.

Once aroused, a motivated, curious individual tends to continue tearing down preconceptions and establishing new connections until a satisfactory outcome materializes, but individuals often operate in circumstances that inhibit such behavior.

Despite her unlikely epiphany about Nixon and her enthusiasm for the film, Elizabeth Deane faced at least three reasons why she couldn't do a documentary on him. First, "It didn't fit into any of the station's ongoing programs," Deane says. "We had a new history series, *The American Experience*, but the general view there was that shows about presidents were boring, and if you looked at what had been done in the past, they were pretty much right." Second, "At that time, in the late 1980s, the men-tion of Nixon's name closed minds—there wasn't a ready audience." And third, "The subject would also make the usual trials of fundraising even more problematic." Yet at the station where Deane works, "Part of the excitement of a project comes from its difficulty—all the better if it goes against the grain of most people's thinking. We want it to say something new, and the support for taking on such a challenge is enormous." For many people, faced with an array of serious frustrations, it would have been easy to shut down the Nixon project. But Deane had encouragement from her boss, vice president for national programming Peter McGhee, who assigned a researcher to work with her, and she had the wherewithal to press on, to honor her motivation for the film. And the support from her station included time, the time necessary to treat obstacles to her project as areas for further problem solving.

With the time and resources of her station behind her, Deane pursued and developed her idea fully, did her research, determined the scope and sequence of her attack, and made a film that was successful in its own right, a film that eventually helped convince the skeptics at *The American Experience* to produce a series of films on American presidents. In the two decades since "Nixon" aired, "The Presidents" has showcased some of *American Experience*'s most acclaimed films, including "LBJ," "FDR," and "Reagan," and has won a George Foster Peabody award—television's highest honor—along with a string of Emmys and Emmy nominations.

This notion, using concerns arising in evaluation as focus areas for more creative work rather than as reasons to abandon the work, is critical to fully realizing a useful creative product. Allowing for this development to happen—providing the time necessary to multiply, reinforce, and verify new connections until they fulfill their promise—is the key to successful evaluation. Sooner or later, one has to make decisions, but new ideas don't come full blown and ready to be accepted or rejected. They need to be explored, modified, and tailored before anyone can make a fair decision about their worth.

Companies that depend entirely on extrinsic motivators like money and position have trouble eliciting new ideas because evaluation of ideas, instead of accommodating further development, usually comes with rapid and rigid application of historically "proven" assumptions. These assumptions rarely nurture creative connection breaking, much less the ideas that come from radically new connections. Successful evaluation needs to allow for time, for the possibility of making mistakes, and even for apparent irrelevance or foolishness.[22]

Evaluation ends with rejection or partial acceptance and further refined search or full acceptance of the idea, at which point the motivation that started and sustains the cycle of creativity ceases. And natural closure allows the active, inquisitive, creative mind to focus on other challenges.

TWO

Becoming Creatively Fit as an Individual

To SUCCESSFULLY CALL on motivation, curiosity and fear, making and breaking connections, and evaluation, you can practice and exercise in those dynamics just as an athlete would. With practice and exercise, you can improve the ability, confidence, and strength you'll need to put the dynamics to their fullest and best use.

A Creative Profile

Before starting any exercises, there is some advice worth thinking about in Sun Tsu's *The Art of War*: "Know your enemy, know yourself."[1]

Know Your Enemy

Be aware of the forces that work against creativity. Most readers will recognize or easily surmise these forces: imitation, conformity, the need to be right immediately, acceptance of fixed roles, paralysis from analysis. Just because they're obvious, though, doesn't mean that they can be disregarded.

What's important to realize is that these forces are not bad in and of themselves. Almost all have value in certain contexts. Imitation is a fantastic way to learn. Conformity can reduce friction, help unify, and foster momentum.[2] Employment contracts and role clarity remove duplication and confusion. Being right early is important in a time-driven world. Rational analysis is essential for quality decisions.

Yet each of these forces can be a serious enemy of creativity. Imitation can quickly become a habit, and once it does, it will keep you from breaking new ground; even the wise practice of benchmarking, a form of imitation, is experienced in some companies as "Don't create. Copy." Close adherence to narrowly described assignments can mean adherence to detrimental assumptions.[3] New ideas rarely come fully formed, and when you try to analyze and decide on their viability right away, you almost inevitably decide too early, killing them before they have a chance to grow into innovative solutions. As an individual, be aware that you can be subject to these forces.

Know Yourself

We suggest that you learn to understand who you are as a creative individual.

Take an inventory of your personal preferences in performing creative work so that you can develop a personal creativity perspective, a creative profile. Then use this profile to assess your creative strengths and weaknesses so that ultimately you do the best creative work you can.

Becoming conscious of your preferences in creative work is a matter of self-observation. Do you perform your best imaginatively when alone, or do you prefer to bounce ideas off others? Do you do your best planning in a favorite spot, or doesn't locale matter? Do you like exploring connections, waiting for one connection that excites you, or immersing yourself in a possible solution and pushing for more ideas on a forward target?

Relevant factors for assessing your profile are outlined here, and in subsequent pages of this chapter we'll discuss how you can enhance your capacity in most of them.

Motivation (particularly intrinsic motivation): Do you know what you want in life? What would you like to be remembered for by those you love? Are you able to align your daily life, work, and career goals with these wants? Are your intrinsic goals stronger than your extrinsic goals?

Curiosity: Do you allow yourself time to follow up on what piques your interest? Do you learn things daily that interest you? Do you have fun every day? Does that fun satisfy you, or does it leave you wanting more? Do you do things just because others do or because you want to be liked?

Management of fear and stress: Are you able to keep fear and stress from running your life? When you're overtaken by anxiety, does it eventually abate enough so that you can have fun again? Are you occasionally able to see the causes of your fears in a humorous light? Are you able to share your new ideas with others, even the half-baked ideas? Can you express your thoughts when they are different from the thoughts of everyone around you?

Connection breaking: Can you accept it when things don't work out the way you thought they might? Can you stand being wrong on the most important issue? Are there places where being wrong is not acceptable to you? Is fantasy acceptable? Can you be silly? Can you tolerate ambiguity when things don't make sense? Can you hold conflicting points of view at the same time, knowing that both might be right?

Connection making: Do you enjoy new ideas, both yours and other people's? Do you like the ideas you get? Can a funny new idea delight you? Can you create five absurd ideas for every problem or opportunity that faces you right now?

Creative evaluation capability: Can you see how most new ideas have merit? Can you see an idea as having parts, some interesting, some good, some that are problem areas? Can you see that every idea can be changed like a menu, varied like clothes, molded like clay? Can you like a new idea even when you see that it might not work?

Self-confidence: Do you think you can find an answer to the problems and opportunities you meet, even if it might take time? Do you think you are creative? Can you listen to ideas from others and use the ideas when you like them and adjust them when you like part of them?

Ability to innovate: Do you feel you can get others to accept your ideas if the ideas are good and if you try hard enough? Do you feel confident enough to accept a compromised idea if acceptance will persuade others to help you make it happen? Do you feel that eventually you can make what's important to you work out?

Reclaiming Creative Health

Now we look at engaging each of the four dynamics. And here, as in considering the pervasive resistance to creativity, it's important to remember how deeply personal and individual creativity is. Keep in mind your own creative profile, know where creativity has been suppressed, know where it still has some muscle, and exercise accordingly. If you're confident of your motivation and know it's your curiosity that's been derailed, you should focus on reviving the curiosity.

We provide a few strengthening exercises for those readers wanting to explore these ideas in more depth. You may not want to do all the exercises in the following sections. That is fine. They are intended as a useful guide, not as an assignment, and are written to provide understanding even if you do not complete them. Take whatever exercises you need, and let them do their work.

Finding Motivation in Personal Vision

Motivation is the first of the creative dynamics. It can drive people into action or it can draw them into action. A heart attack drives a libertine to adopt a drastically new approach to physical health. This is extrinsic motivation. A career, on the other hand, might become a calling that draws an individual to the particular performance of a job. Many people, from police officers to senators, from investment bankers to teachers, feel deeply that what they do matters. They make sacrifices to do what they do in the way they feel it must be done. These people don't do the work because they're driven by circumstance. They do the work because they're drawn to it.

The beat cop whose career is a calling doesn't just patrol; from natural as well as professional curiosity, he learns about his blocks and the people who live and work in them. He develops relationships and participates in the spirit and history of the place. His life becomes part of the life of his beat and vice versa. Along with the occasional pain and violence, he shares in the joy, the adventure, the fun. He learns to rap with the kids' music on the corner and knows which kids are going wrong and what's become of their families. He knows the vibe outside the bar on Friday and his place in the vibe and can put the two together in a way that keeps the end of the week harmonious. And he likes this. He wants to do it, despite the possible danger from criminal activity.

This is intrinsic motivation, at the heart of which is personal vision. Psychologist Robert Fritz uses a rubber band to illustrate the power of a personal vision.[4] Imagine a rubber band stretched between two hands. Feel the tension; the rubber band is trying to contract. Now imagine that the hand at one end of the band represents vision and hand at the other end represents everyday life. If the vision is strong and fixed, that hand, that end of the rubber band, will stay where it is, no matter what. Everyday life, however, is constantly in flux, so there will be moments when the pressures of circumstance subside and the hand that holds the daily end of the rubber band will be drawn toward the vision hand by the rubber band's tension. This is a rubber band where the tension never relaxes to permit daily life to increase its separation from vision, so over time, the rubber band will draw changeable life, whatever its occasional frustrations, inexorably closer to alignment with the steady vision.

Through his metaphor, Fritz illustrates that a powerful vision draws and aligns life with itself, overcoming obstacles to the vision. And as vision is at the heart of intrinsic motivation, a more powerful vision will make intrinsic motivation stronger, more apparent, more immune to the wear of everyday life.

The vision doesn't have to be grand. For a ten-year-old who wants to play in the majors, professional baseball is the vision. Thus practice after school is not just practice, it serves the calling, the vision. The vision often evolves in degree of importance and can coexist with other visions. In college the baseball player may discover a passion for mathematics that becomes a governing vision for his lifetime. He hasn't lost baseball, but what pulls and orients life to him is the mathematics. His desire for a mate will add magnetism and orientation to another area of his life. All three visionary poles, in their time and sphere, constitute the core of intrinsic motivation and the potential initiation of creativity. Even though this may seem obvious, it's no less important. The problem comes when vision subsides and with it, the intrinsic motivation so important to the creative process.

So where does one get a personal vision? You can't manufacture vision when it's not there. If vision has been lost, you uncover it among intentions and goals set aside during the passages of life. This search for the essential elements of personal vision is itself a motivator. The search to learn what matters most deeply to you will itself help revitalize your creative thought.

How do you go about this search for personal vision? Use the following exercises as a start. At least a few of the exercises here and throughout this chapter have to do not only with business but with life outside business. We include them, even knowing that readers may be tempted to consider them irrelevant, because they are important. In thousands of meetings with clients over the years, we have constantly seen new work-related ideas forming as people drew on their nonwork interests—gardening, browsing in hardware stores, attending church, cooking, heliskiing, parenting, building kayaks. All parts of life are part of the deep reserve people tap into for the connections that help create new and useful ideas for business.

Exercises: Searching for Personal Vision

1. During the course of your day, look for three things that might represent you—first as you were at ten years old, second as who you are today, and third as who you are at your absolute best. Write a sentence about how each representation relates to you. Do this several times. Look for patterns—what do they tell you?

   A day at this exercise might produce something like this:

   First I saw a baseball in a store window and remembered the father-and-son baseball game I played on Memorial Day weekend when I was ten. For me, this represents the fun of being on teams and being both competitive and friendly.

   Then I saw a vine at the corner of the house next door and it reminded me of a gardener saying about vines, "First year they sleep; second year they creep; third year they leap." The vine and the gardener's adage speak to the fact that my most important work now won't come to fruition for several years, and I ought to try not be discouraged by the paucity of visible results right now.

Finally, a fountain with multiple jets seemed to represent my desire to keep coming up with something new from what I already have and also to represent the beauty of how that newness can work with other people doing the same thing.

After several iterations, patterns will begin to appear. Examine them for how you know yourself in terms of creativity, how you might envision yourself performing creatively. It may become apparent, extending this example, that you're deeply motivated to succeed with others. As you understand this and see the pattern continue, you can think about how it might apply to your future creative efforts. You might look to others to be your trigger for new ideas, rather than feeling required to create by yourself. This sort of perspective can free you (or anybody else) for literally hundreds of sources of stimulation each day.

2. Write what we call a "future memory" article. This is an article about you, in a magazine you respect, in a field of your interest, written as if it were five years from now. The article describes events occurring between today and five years from now. Here are the guidelines:

   - Describe a moment celebrating something important you've accomplished, five years from now, in an area important to you.

   - Write with rich detail about the future. Visualize what's happening.

   - Note key decisions five years ago (today) that made the success possible.

   - Report what the subject of the article, you, imagine doing for the next five years.

   - Don't worry about the quality of the prose; get the story down and vividly, in about three or four paragraphs.

You might write something like this:

March 20, 2009, issue of Business Week—*Dateline Paris.*
   MegaBank announced that Jack Cigliani has received the prestigious Community Innovation Award for the most successful new

service to strengthen the ties of the bank to the community. His program, called MicroArt, promotes the development of profit-making arts programs. Through micro loans and volunteer consulting of the staff, the bank has now helped 175 arts organizations across the country to be more self-sustaining.

This program is not only profitable to the bank, but it has also strengthened the bank's relationship to the community and proven to be a model for a dozen other corporations. When asked how the idea came about, Mr. Cigliani said, "I had previously worked for the World Bank as it was providing micro loans to developing countries and saw how powerful that approach was. Privately, I have always loved singing, have been in a choir, and have always seen what a struggle it is for these groups to earn enough to keep going. So one night I had the idea to invent a new type of capital—Art Capital. First we would get a bank to grant a loan to the group and to provide the opportunity for members of the bank to consult on a pro bono basis to help the business side of the group. In addition to paying back the loan, the group has the responsibility to provide a return on Art Capital—to do something spectacular for the bank's employees, such as a concert or art for the hallways. I brought the idea to my current bank and they supported me through the many ups and downs to get to where we are."

In giving the award, Jack Bucks, CEO of MegaBank, lauded Cigliani's work. "MegaBank has become large by staying small. We know we live and work in many communities and must stay intimately connected with them. Mr. Cigliani connected his dreams to the dreams of his bank and the dreams of his community. We are all the beneficiaries."

When Mr. Cigliani was asked what he would be doing five years from now, he reflected, "What I know is important to me is making a real difference where I work and not have that separated from the rest of my life. Connecting those two was the driver for Art Capital. Right now I want to see if I can invent other forms of capital that would allow our organization to tap into the best and brightest thinkers on financial instruments without having them on our staff. Perhaps it is bringing us full circle to barter—a sort of intellectual barter."

The "future memory" exercise uses your imagination to help you be explicit about what you want to accomplish. Envisioning outside your range will help you create possibilities that, while currently impractical, invite deeper speculation that can in turn trigger other insights about the nature of your vision and how to achieve it. To allay the fears of senior managers who are concerned that personal vision work might encourage employees to leave for other careers, we can report that we've found that most people don't discover a motivation to run golf schools. They want to make a difference where they are, in the work and life they've established.

Fortifying to Protect Curiosity

Curiosity and fear often come hand in hand, but it is curiosity that furthers creativity. There is real value to creativity in inoculation against the distractions of fear, especially for people who feel that their curiosity is not what it could be.

Harvard Business School professor Teresa Amabile worked with children to inoculate them against the loss of their creative talent, especially the loss of curiosity.[5] She engaged kids in problems where creative thought, especially the vulnerable openness of curiosity, was needed for finding the solution. Amabile then interrupted each session with requests designed to inhibit curiosity. She cut off speculative exploration, set unreasonable deadlines, required a perfect solution. Each of these demands imposes stunting anxiety—fear—on relaxed and actively curious individuals, whether children or adults.

At the end of each session Amabile talked with the class about how they had handled the exercise. If the children did not bring up her interruptions to the exercise, she did. Through discussing the negative influences to creativity, Amabile was inoculating the kids against the fear-inducing frustrations that life offers creativity in general and curiosity in particular. Her goal was to help the children discover what it feels like to be creative, what gets in the way, and how to maintain an open, curious, creative state of mind.

Can an adult inoculate him- or herself against the loss of curiosity? Yes. By continually, in measured doses, exposing yourself to the unknown in its various forms, you build up an increasing resistance to the fear of it, you stem the fight-or-flight urge, and you build a correspondingly greater ability to be confidently open to the new.

Annie Gaudreault at Russell Branding wanted to overcome her innate, as she saw it, alienation from creativity and from the company's creative team. A self-described "suit who comes from a long line of business people,"[6] Gaudreault managed client accounts for seven years before becoming managing director.

It was the less creative side of the business, but I worked with the best creative people, and it became a personal goal to learn how they work. Our president helped me understand and respect the differences between creative and business types, and the conditions the designers need to work. He still catches me whenever I'm being a bureaucrat, and we talk about other ways I can manage the business. I've read everything I can about creativity, and now I see it as part of me, too. I live in both worlds.

Initially a creative cipher, Gaudreault regularly and consciously thrust herself into the creative mix. Gradually, by degrees, she overcame her alienation from the "unknown" creative process and discovered an affinity for it. She still wouldn't call herself creative, but the exposure allowed her to open herself sympathetically, with genuine curiosity, and productively to the once foreign needs and gifts of the creative people around her. Gaudreault has successfully inoculated herself against the inhibitions of what she considered her uncreative nature.

As inoculation takes effect, inhibitions recede. The weaker the inhibitions, the more chance for even the slightest motivation to spark more investigation.

Exercises to Encourage Curiosity

1. Look back over the last month. What was most enjoyable and satisfying in your professional life? Was it the nature of the work, the
way you attacked it, its importance, the intensity required, the
prospect of success? What conversations about the work were
most exciting? Use these questions to reacquaint yourself with the
sense of your own curiosity. Notice what it feels like to wonder
about something that interests and pleases you.

    Now recall any moments in the past month when you had this
same feeling, felt your curiosity activated about something other
than your immediate professional responsibilities. Whether or not
you can recall any such moment, stay alert in the days ahead for
moments when you feel the pull of curiosity drawing you away
from whatever you are doing. Instead of refocusing on your work
at this point, allow your curiosity more time. Call it daydreaming or
what you will; a few minutes of it won't irreparably harm your performance and might very well help it.

    When you have time at the end of the day, reflect on what
captured your curiosity. What did the extra time you allowed the
curiosity give you? Was it fun? What did you learn? Can you now
remember other daydreams that became part of your conscious
and productive thinking? Can you imagine this process of encouraging curiosity becoming part of your thinking in the future?

    For the next week continue to allow yourself a few extra min-
utes a day to see where your apparently idle curiosity leads.
Remember those places. Write them down, if you like, when recol-
lecting them at the end of the day. Not only will you see that you
receive useful news about the work you're doing, you will see your
curiosity grow in range and strength. And you yourself will become
more comfortable with the way your curiosity operates, confident
of its productivity, and more able to release it at will.

2. When fear gets in the way of curiosity, subject the fear to the following Socratic questions.

- What is the evidence for this fear?

- Is this always true?

- Has this been true in the past?

- What are the odds of this really happening (or being true)?

- What is the very worst that could happen? What is so bad about that? What would I do if the worst happened?

- Am I looking at the whole picture?

- Am I being fully objective?[7]

3. Imagine that you've been given the assignment of running a division that is in serious trouble and needs to be turned around. You don't know if you can turn it around, and even if you can, it may be sold off before you have a chance to give it your best shot. Ask yourself questions that acknowledge the cause of your anxiety and that also make it concrete, something you can deal with, rather than an amorphous knot in your stomach. How lacking can your abilities be if you've been handed the assignment? How bad is the division, and what exactly has to happen for a turnaround? What are the odds of the division being sold and when, and how does that change if you make progress? What happens if you're around only long enough to get blamed for the mess?

Not all of these questions will be comfortable to ask or to answer, but having them out in the open can take away the anxiety of the unknown and give you the chance to address the cause of the anxiety in practical ways.

Breaking Connections

Breaking old connections leads to new connections and creative ideas. To break old connections, first search out the assumptions that contain the old connections. Assumptions are often invisible, often what everyone "knows" as fundamental truth underlying the circumstance in question. Examine these assumptions for flaws. Dare them not to be true. "Nixon was reprehensible and no one wants to hear about him ever again." "Nobody can walk into color, and color has nothing whatever to do with reassuring vulnerable users of HR software." "Once a furniture maker, always a furniture maker."

Then discard the assumption to break the connection it embodies. Nixon may not be altogether damaged, and it may not be true that no one wants to hear about him. Maybe people can walk into color, and maybe color can reassure people. Maybe a furniture maker is not always only a furniture maker, so maybe furniture is not the whole story.

Exercises for Connection Breaking

1. List your most certain assumptions about the following:

   • Your company. For example, "Any serious competition will come from current players within the industry because established relationships are so deep and so important."

   • Your position. For example, "I cannot handle another major innovation without more resources on staff."

   • Your division. "Our job is to enact strategy, not to change it."

   Imagine that you've just found out that each of these assumptions has been proven not true. Create plausible explanations, such as what new competitor arrived on the scene, what enabled you to handle an increased workload, and so on.

   The idea here is to recognize assumptions, to understand the possibility that you can in fact break them. It's always easier to recognize assumptions you know to be assumptions, rather than ones that are embedded, perhaps hidden, as absolute truth. It's also easier to contemplate breaking them in the abstract when consequences have less immediacy. With practice, you will be confident moving out of the abstract.

2. Talk in depth to someone with whom you disagree deeply on a matter of importance. Listen to his view. Try to understand his view and the background that brings him to it. Imagine yourself holding this view. How does the world change for you?

3. Imagine yourself as another person who holds your current position. Take time to imagine in detail arriving for work today as a mother, a sailor, a blind man, a crook, a writer gathering information. How do your routines change with each perspective? How do your responsibilities change?

Between Breaking and Making Connections: Practicing Purposeful Confusion

The instant an individual breaks a powerful connection, new and perhaps useful connections can be made. Intuition about the new connections may in fact persuade the individual to leave the old connection permanently broken.

Sometimes you might find yourself uncomfortably between connections, which is to say without the old certainty and without a new one—confused. Try to get used to the confusion. Stay in it. Resist the urge to resolve it. Confusion and anxiety are integral to creativity; you almost always have to break the old flawed connection before fully recognizing and making new and improved connections. Practice saying, "I don't know."

While John Gibson was CEO at Landmark Graphics, a large software firm in the oil industry, he and his staff found themselves unsure about a solution they had come up with just as they were about to implement it. "I was at a meeting where a team was discussing how to implement . . . , and I had to say, 'I don't know exactly what we're doing . . . what problem we're solving.'"[8]

In response to a problem, the group had already worked their way past some inhibiting assumptions and were eager to put a solution in place. But they started talking about the problem and in doing so brought up a lot of other possible problems, including some they knew were not part of the immediate issue but that might relate to it. "We were hunting the real problem," Gibson explained, "and that's very different from solving the problem." Although the team had already reached the point of implementation, they were able to step back, spend time "not knowing," and eventually come up with a more fundamental problem and a broader, more profound solution.

When you break an old connection, you will naturally want a new one in a hurry. Be aware that the best connections may not come quickly. Practicing purposeful confusion, tolerating profound and long-lasting ambiguity, allows the best connections to surface, perhaps redefining the original construct or beliefs so that even the perception of the problem alters.

Embracing purposeful confusion, tolerating the ambiguity before solution, gets easier with practice. Remaining in this netherworld leads to richer and more far-flung connections when they finally do form.

Exercise in Purposeful Confusion

There is a storytelling exercise we use for practicing tolerance not just to routine ambiguity but to ambiguity loaded with absurdity and discontinuity. There's nothing routine or predictable about what happens when the potent connections of a deeply held assumption break. It can be disconcertingly absurd and frighteningly unpredictable.

It works best with a group, but in theory, you could do the exercise alone. One person starts making up a story, an absurd story. During the middle of this absurd story the next person inserts a major discontinuity. Each person in the group adds to the story.

As you make up and pass along the story, you will probably feel, at first anyway, ill at ease with the absurdity and nonetheless anxious to make sense of the discontinuities. As the exercise continues, you will become more at ease with both and feel free to let the stories unfold as they will. This willingness to accept and allow the uneasy absurdity and nervous disconnection, the deep ambiguity that follows broken connections, is surprisingly useful for staying the course to make new connections that may prove even more absurd than your stories.

> *A bug walks down the street, enjoying the sun and the day, avoiding the shoes slapping down on all sides. He learned about shoes in bug school. Bug school is generally three hours long, a significant part of a bug's life. Anyway, the sunlight is showing dust eddies, which look suspiciously regular to the bug. Five hours later the bug is presenting his hypothesis to man and bug alike: "The regularity of dust eddies in sunbeams: Proof of God or Brownian inevitability?" By the time he wins the Nobel Prize for his work, he's been dead for 2,500 generations.*

At this point, the first storyteller hands the story off to the next person in the group, who must carry it on to the point of inserting another discontinuity of a different sort.

> *The bug had 40 million descendents at the Nobel ceremony, which this year was held at ten-year-old Billy Smith's birthday party in Sandusky, Ohio . . .*

Practice acceptance of absurdity as connections break down. Embrace it as you search for new connections.

Making Connections

Connection making comes naturally. You hear a strange noise and you create an explanation for it. You're handed a menu in a language you cannot read and yet manage one way or another to order what you want. Every day people wrestle order from the confusion of incoming information.

The ease of filling in the blank, putting together new and old information, belies the importance of actively exercising the ability to connect. Connections are the wellspring of creative thought, and the more consciously you practice opening your mind to make connections, the better you will be at making them and the more you will make them.

Making a greater number of connections isn't just a probability game in the hope that one connection will make it past some threshold of acceptability. Rather, when you understand with deep confidence that an infinite number of connections and subsequent ideas exist, you don't need to be unduly attached to any one of them.

Doug Farmer, an engineer at an American oil company, was looking for ways to reduce the costs of construction on a new refinery that would produce the full range of petroleum distillates. It was a perennial problem, and Farmer felt he needed an innovative approach. Trying to get a grip on the cost cutting, Farmer imagined the flow of crude oil as it entered the refinery, before it went through the various processes of reduction to emerge as separate gas and oil products. As Farmer explained,

I wanted to think about flow in a different way. The flow of traffic came to mind. I tried to forget about refining petroleum and just pictured myself standing in the middle of a wide street, about six lanes one way. I could look down the street in my mind and see, a quarter mile away, six cars stopped at a light. The light changed, and all six cars started. They were all coming in my direction. By the time the traffic had gotten to me, two of the cars had pulled off to park, and two others had turned corners; only two of the original cars passed me, one on each side. As I sat there thinking about those cars, wondering what the flow of traffic had to do with the flow of oil in a refinery, I got an idea. Suppose an initial cracking vessel could separate out huge portions of crude oil and shunt them off to one of our already-built refineries, like the cars that turned off onto another street. Then we could take what was left—the better, really expensive portion of the crude—and build a smaller specialty refinery for it. I spent much of the night working on drawings of how this could happen.[9]

Usually, when people are asked to think about the flow of oil, they compare it to the flow of other liquids—"like water, only thicker." This kind of thinking accounts for the current design of refineries. By making a more far-fetched connection through dreamlike imagining, Farmer arrived at a new idea about the flow of oil that could save his company a lot of money.

The odds are low that the first idea for any problem or opportunity will be the best solution, so keep going. Get to the most fanciful ideas and come up with ten of them, dream up fifty, trying to be more fanciful, more far-fetched as you go. As the ideas mount, each one becomes less precious and faces less pressure to be a perfect idea. Collectively they offer a wide range of potential alternative courses of action. Abundance of ideas and richness of speculation make the best pool from which to choose the most useful connections.

As Shakespeare advised: "There are more things in heaven and earth than are dreamt of in your philosophy."[10] Go find some of them.

Exercises for Connection Making

1. Think of two related fields, such as music and painting, and list a few connections between them. Each is an art; each can be said to have color and flow; each elicits a personal vision. Now make similar connections between more disparate objects, such as the sun and a desk stapler. Atoms, shine, what else? Now raise the stakes and do some time trials: How many connections can you find between, say, a bottle of water and a computer in 90 seconds? As you go, try to make ever more interesting and provocative connections.

   You will discover, as many people do, that you have a near-infinite ability to find connections between apparently unconnected things. Understand that you have this ability and practice it, and you will prepare yourself to make creative connections when purposefully pursuing the creative process.

Eventually, you will make connections that are rich with confusion, uncertainty, anxiety and ambiguity—as well as possibility. This probably will be uncomfortable at first. Expect this discomfort. It is a price of playing the game. You will discover very little creativity in yourself without the discomfort of confusion, uncertainty, anxiety, and ambiguity.

The following exercise is a storytelling variation.

2. On your own or with a group, think of fifteen completely different uses for newspaper: lining a cat litter tray, swatting mosquitoes, making paper airplanes, reading, cutting out words to make notes. Next list things for which a newspaper could never be used, such as a trampoline or a lawnmower. Now look over the impossibilities and see if there is any way at all newspaper could in fact be used. Imagine the absurd or the obvious. Maybe newspaper would serve as a trampoline for fleas. If you laminated the paper, you could use it as a sort of scythe. Reach farther. Make a lot of connections and make them wilder and wilder.

Remember, with connections, you want to keep pushing for more and you want to keep pushing farther afield. Range in connections is what will lead to new and successful ideas.

Evaluation and Reflection

There is a common, irrational fear that the longer a goal goes unmet or a problem unsolved, the more impossible the goal gets and the worse the problem. As always, fear inhibits creativity. At the end of the creative process, this fear expresses itself in the rush to judgment.

When people first break old connections, they feel an urgency to make the new connections. We urge you instead to try and embrace purposeful confusion. When people feel they have the new connections in hand, when they feel they have the problem correctly identified and the creative goal all but accomplished, they feel only greater urgency to confirm those connections and get on with the implementation.

Avoid rushing to judgment by keeping your connections from solidifying too early. One method is to identify a deadline before which you will not reach a final decision and to plan for slack in the schedule as the deadline approaches.

Paul Dietrich, a former principal at the award-winning architectural firm Cambridge Seven Associates, explained the process in his firm.

> *When we have an interesting project, our behavior seems to follow a certain pattern. A couple of weeks before the deadline for the drawings and the final proposal, the designers wander the hallways, sometimes talking to each other, sometimes looking out the window. There is increased activity, but none of that activity is directed at anything. Then a couple of days before the proposal is due, everybody gathers to determine the best approach and pull it together. We've learned over the years that delay is crucial to the way work happens around here.*[11]

Laura Wills describes the pulse of delay in creating design at Russell Branding.

> *Typically we start projects as a group, getting the right people together for a major briefing, and then scatter. Some of us go to strategize, others to work on drawings. Sometimes people go out and walk around the city. Days later we get back together to share our thoughts, then scatter again, then regroup again. After several cycles we've settled on the best new ideas and are ready to go to the client.*[12]

Often a truly new idea needs more than just the grace of time for evaluation; it needs kindness.

David Perkins, professor at Project Zero, the center for the study of human cognitive potential at Harvard University, agreed to meet with a young man who wanted to explain a complicated new idea. Perkins chose a restaurant near his office as a meeting place, knowing that a traditional academic office might be intimidating for a first "exposure." He sat and listened attentively while the young man presented his idea in full. After asking a few clarifying questions, Perkins sat quietly for awhile, occasionally making notes or staring off into space as he sorted through the idea. When he was ready, Perkins launched into an analysis of all the benefits of the idea, made constructive connections to other concepts, and suggested additional theories to back up the idea. By the time Perkins got around to his concerns, which were serious, the young man was able to hear them as areas to work on rather than reasons to quit. The entire conversation took less than forty minutes and added a richness to the original idea that would not have been possible otherwise.[13]

How does this work when evaluating your own idea? If you know you've made a tenuous but potentially successful connection, you should evaluate it honestly but with a sympathetic method like the one Perkins used, first searching out all the positive aspects and interesting connections and only later examining the drawbacks.

In evaluation, as in every other dynamic of the creative process, individual style matters enormously. Pay attention to your own creative profile, become familiar with when and where you're likely to judge too quickly and too harshly, know when you've given sufficient attention to every idea.

Exercises for Evaluation

1. Identify a problem or opportunity for which you have several ideas. Write one of the ideas at the head of a sheet of paper and list at least four benefits of using the idea as your answer to the problem or your way to best seize the opportunity. Do the same with another idea, one you are less confident or excited about. After seeing the benefits, do you feel any friendlier to the second idea?

On the surface, it seems a silly question. Do I feel any friendlier? Yet many people do, illustrating a phenomenon: People usually evaluate so quickly and so harshly that often they're not even aware of the parts of an idea they like. The friendliness reflects a more realistic discovery or recognition of the good parts of an idea. Skilled creators learn to build on the good elements of an idea and move away from the problem elements.

Now turn to a problem for which you have only poor ideas. Put one of those ideas at the head of a page and list at least four benefits for using it. Do the same with several other poor ideas.

You may not feel any friendlier to the lousy ideas, although most people find they do. At the very least, your patient and positive examination of the lousy ideas will have strengthened the discipline you'll need to avoid rushing to judgment. At best, you have begun to gain confidence in the understanding that any ideas, even apparently bad ones, have interesting possibilities.

Now do it all with a problem or opportunity that has only off-the-wall ideas for solution or attack. By this time, you should have begun to absorb the essential ethos of evaluation: Examine the most unlikely ideas with patience and with readiness to be surprised by success.

Most of us have erected effective mental mechanisms that automatically scan incoming ideas and cull them before too much is "wasted" in useless thought. Thus, only the immediately-recognized-as-important ideas get full recognition, much less examination. This is useful for efficient thinking, but for creativity it is in fact wasteful censorship. To be creatively fit, you need to become aware that we all overlook potentially useful ideas. This awareness helps to break the habit of automatic sorting and rejection. The process of creative transformation uses the initially unseen benefits of apparently poor ideas to lead to new thinking generally and to practical, purposeful thinking about specific creative solutions.

Evaluation is a dynamic for building and growing, for appreciating and nurturing ideas, for trying to see how new and untried ideas might just possibly work. Quick judgment, even arbitrarily quick judgment in favor of one early idea, denies the possibilities creativity generates.

2. Take a page from debate teams. Argue one of your sacred cows from the opponent's position. Doing so helps you appreciate the stretch in your mind and, with practice, makes quick, presumptive judgments less automatic.

   The fact that you have spent time learning to recognize and refute assumptions makes it easier for you to spot and set aside the same sorts of assumptions that can lead to abrupt and self-defeating judgments during what should be the period of encouraging evaluation.

   Each of the dynamics in the creative process is as engaging individually as the entire creative process. You the individual are the critical variable in both the process and its parts. The individual who wants to be fit and successful creatively will practice and while practicing will become as deeply aware as possible of what he or she brings to the process in terms of personal strengths and weaknesses.

THREE

Breaking and Making Connections for an Enterprise

THE DYNAMICS OF CREATIVITY apply to companies as well as individuals, but a company is more than a metaphor for a person; variables of complexity, scale, and environment come into play; other individuals come into play. In a company, motivation, curiosity, and evaluation are nurtured greatly by the corporate climate, and we'll discuss climate in the next section of the book.

Breaking and making connections, the pivotal dynamic of the creative process, has a distinct and special utility among the creative dynamics. Because of that, we devote an entire chapter to it. We use the Steelcase Inc. story both to illustrate the importance of breaking and making connections and as a background example of specific corporate practice. Then, in subsequent pages, we discuss general principles that will help other companies in other circumstances break and make their own connections.

In the introduction, remember, we related that Steelcase's R&D had discovered that the company's new products were not well differentiated from those of its competitors. In addition, the market was changing so quickly and dramatically that the entire industry was losing touch with its customers. Steelcase needed to rethink the office furniture business and its relationship to that business. The company started this rethinking ten years ago and came up with the understanding that furniture is part of a larger system, that it needs to be integrated into office "pathways," the umbilical cord of utilities and capabilities upon which offices depend. "That was the start," according to Mark Greiner, vice president of R&D. "We have now evolved the pathways framework to include three domains: architecture, the envelope of space; furniture, the objects within that space; and technology, which provides capability. The solutions we build must depend on the seamless integration of those three domains. The research triggered by this framework is still mushrooming—there are plenty of unexplored areas."

As the pathways framework was beginning to connect Steelcase to new possibilities of business solutions, James Hackett, the Steelcase CEO, made another connection. Much of the company's traditional strength came from its customer relationships, and Hackett became deeply interested in how Steelcase might build on those relationships and use the power of observational science to serve the customer in new ways. Hackett started studying the techniques of anthropologists and sociologists and encouraged R&D to embark on experiments in direct observation. As Greiner relates:

An early experiment was to install cameras in the ceilings of some of our [customers'] spaces and observe how people used the environment. What we saw were patterns—people struggling to work around what wasn't working for them—trying to manage their space and their privacy in an open environment. Often these tapes gave us information a customer would never tell us in words. They would never say, for example, that they "always moved stuff around to provide some barrier between themselves and their open doorways," but over and over the tapes would show one person putting a chair just so, and another person a plant—invariably providing some privacy or protection. Or that they would orient the office or themselves so their backs were never blindly exposed to the doorways. But the tapes showed these patterns clearly.

Steelcase's growing explorations in these two directions, pathways and direct observation, kept expanding. What further developments were on the way in technology and architecture? How would those developments affect people? How would the evolving purposes and tasks of people affect the spaces? What would it all mean in terms of furniture?

Leadership quickly moved beyond the company's traditional commitment to making pieces of furniture. Steelcase researchers thought in the broadest possible terms about the way space could be used and configured. They began to study sociological aspects of dyadic work versus team or individual work; they studied the psychological aspects of creative spaces and focused and learning spaces; they studied the ergonomics of anatomical supports for workers and the constant shift of desk-person-chair minute-by-minute through the day.

Greiner elaborates:

One thing we explored was mobility. We started by putting wheels on everything. But the next connection was that furniture must reconfigure around people in constant motion; the furniture itself must be in constant flex. Our observations showed that, even when seated, people are in constant motion, and our anatomical study showed how the entire body changes throughout the day as muscles tire. One result of this research was a series of chairs that automatically move with the user, maintaining back support no matter how you sit in them. One of these, the Leap chair, became one of the top-selling chairs in the world the year of its introduction. And taking the larger office and the idea of flex and people's observed needs to personalize their space, we have identified ways to make all our solutions, and so far we have identified 23 quadrillion points of option, to configure exactly to each user.

Steelcase's expansion into the pathways orientation around technology led them to connect with IBM. IBM, in turn, was excited by Steelcase's strength in observational research. The recent unveiling of Steelcase and IBM's experimental "Blue-Space," with multiple modes for information flow and maximum flexibility to make technology configure to the user in constant motion, demonstrates the promise of making technology as well as space and furniture adapt to people, instead of the other way around. "Here too," Greiner says, "we've barely scratched the surface of possibilities."

Chasing a new concept of the workspace—completing the break with the old business model and making valid connections into a new model—began with individual leaders.

Jack Tanis, director of user and field research, remodeled his office following design principles of modern suburban kitchens because "the kitchen is one of the most functional areas in a house and the most conducive to conversation."[1] He tracked how people's interaction and focus changed as they moved around his new office space, and noted how different configurations encouraged formal, casual, or experimental kinds of thinking and relating. His observations led to new approaches in the design and integration of desks and filing systems and the space they occupied.

Manager Dave Lathrop realized employees and clients of this traditional furniture manufacturer had to be taught how to think, along with the company's leaders, about space as a critical design element. And they had to be taught on the fly. So he explored theories of learning-through-application in order to find the best way to educate both employees and clients as the company continued to do business during the transition to a new business model.

These sorts of efforts encouraged and coalesced into a companywide creative revolution at Steelcase.

With projects that director Rick Mohr called "bugs-to-light," company leaders brought disparate groups of people together for creative connectionmaking around the evolving business model. These were projects designed to stimulate and inform the creative professionals from all areas of the company. These gifted participants then took back to their departments the understanding and enthusiasm they'd gained about the new business model and about the creative work involved in both the transition to that model and the ongoing practice of the new business. One such project involves staff, customers, and outside experts meeting periodically to focus on unique solutions for specific customer problems. Thinking and working directly with customers allows Steelcase teams to try out and quickly refine solutions at customer sites, which become real-time laboratories for field testing.

To complete the break from traditional manufacture and to advertise, to embody, the switch to new business possibilities, senior executives opened up the top corporate floor, which housed about sixty people, into one room, eliminating private offices. In an experiment they called "displayed thinking," the executives each kept all of their current projects on white boards or flip charts near their desks. The desks were arranged so officers had to pass one another's work regularly. Jim Keene, former senior vice president and now CFO, explains that the arrangement not only helped drive the company through its turn to the new direction, but also institutionalized the new creative ethos necessary to maintain that direction.

> *There is big-C creativity, the breakthrough kind, and small-c creativity, the everyday kind. Small-c creativity, where 90 percent of new stuff comes from, emerges from the environment people find themselves in every day. I make new connections in my thinking just by noticing what's in my environment when I walk around. When we enrich the environment, we get even more of the kind of creative thinking we want.[2]*

As Mark Greiner relates, Steelcase looked outward as well. "Observing how critical persistent information is to business, and building on our 'displayed thinking' activity, we purchased Poly-Vision, which made both standard and digital whiteboards. And we threw ourselves into the study of presentation." A result of this strategy is the new Steelcase Huddleboard, a mobile presentation system that consists of several lightweight markerboards and a framework that allows for work, storage, mobility, and display. The whole system, including several markerboards, weighs less than five pounds and gives a person the ability to prepare a complex presentation and carry it to wherever the audience is.

Steelcase moved aggressively from being a self-described "insulated Midwestern furniture manufacturer" to being an open-ended experimental laboratory for innovation, intent on keeping ahead of the way people work. Ultimately, the business was brand new, from strategy through sales. It had moved from a product base of tangible items of furniture to spatial solutions for the workplace with furniture as an accompaniment to the solution. Creativity in the company had expanded from a single, traditional design department to a companywide creative capability for anticipating and answering rapid evolution in total workplace needs.

Steelcase turned itself around using every dynamic in the creative process. But the pivotal dynamic was first and foremost the breaking and making of connections. Steelcase found that its longstanding assumptions about its industry and its own business were out of touch with how quickly work was changing. In order to thrive, Steelcase had to discard those assumptions and develop new ideas about what it did and what it could do. It broke the connections to traditional manufacturing and made new connections to current ideas about space and about the designing of work environments.

Companies in different circumstances may follow entirely different paths into and through the creative process. Sooner or later, however, every company will need to break and make connections.

The Steelcase story is a specific example of the potential creativity holds for positive metamorphosis. Now we'll work step by step through the component elements of breaking and making connections so that other companies can engage this critical dynamic.

Companies build articulated and unarticulated mental maps of their relationships, their markets, their social or political interests, whatever is relevant to the pursuit of their business. The maps serve to organize a company's world and to block out extraneous, disorienting information. They allow a company to act efficiently and to predict business outcomes accurately. They also, however, blind companies not only to other possibilities but also to clues that the world outside the map may be changing and that the map itself may be losing accuracy.

Steelcase discovered that the market didn't want to simply buy furniture anymore. Customers needed a complete environmental solution. The company was operating with what had become an outdated map of its business. And when Napster built a mechanism for its members to share music among themselves for nothing, the music industry was shocked. Never having used a mental map other than a supply-and-demand retail chain distribution model, the industry was stumped as to how to respond effectively to the new peer-to-peer trading model, even after Napster itself faded from the scene.

When a familiar map breaks down, or when a company discards the map, there's terrific uncertainty as old connections cease and new ones form. And the more dependent a company's livelihood on the accuracy of its map, on the efficacy of its old connections, the more disturbing the fracture of those connections. But the fracture and the subsequent passage to new connections can be managed securely, if not always comfortably, through performance of a set of several key actions.

The keys to successfully embracing the challenge and opportunity of breaking and making corporate connections lie in encouraging conflict and risk taking, in promoting diversity, in organizing groups to tap intrinsic motivation, and in encouraging the flow of information throughout the enterprise.

Encourage Conflict of Ideas

Conflict is a rich yet tricky vein to mine. Conflict between different ideas and points of view can be instrumental in breaking down established connections and generating new material for new connections for useful new solutions. Creative organizations encourage a measure of internal conflict precisely because the conflict can challenge and break up entrenched ways of thinking and promote new ideas.[3]

Yet, as well as aiding connection breaking, conflict can easily raise levels of fear, lower motivation, shut down connection making, distort evaluation, and damage climate. Because of the way the conflict occurs, people experience it as personal conflict rather than conflict of ideas. To increase the likelihood of getting the benefits without the disturbances, there are a few guidelines. The first is to take care that the parties involved understand the intent of the conflict.

Parties in productive conflict need to believe that the intent is to create a better idea together. This means quite consciously getting past a win-lose approach in which argument takes place on the plane of "Our idea's good, yours is flawed, I need to defend our idea and myself."[4]

Often, the negative aspect of conflict arises around evaluation that is experienced as evaluation of character, such as "You are flawed because your idea is flawed." George Prince, founder of Synectics, describes the law of discount revenge that results from this often unconscious leap from the idea to the person. "If I am discounted as a person, I will get revenge, somehow, sometime—it may not even be conscious, but I'll get it. So if I view the conflict, the evaluation, as a discounting of me, part of my creative energy is then devoted to finding a socially acceptable way of getting even."[5] The law of discount revenge is not valuable to creativity.

Productive intent can partly be established by designating problem solvers to evaluate and give guidance for further work to other colleagues in the creative effort. Instead of self-appointed individuals saying "Let me be the devil's advocate" simply to support their idea, a conflict leader can be chosen by the group to impartially focus on any missing elements in the thinking of the group as a whole. We do not recommend conflict for conflict's sake alone. Encourage participants toward twofold curiosity: about potential flaws in an idea and about ways to deal with flaws.

Separating conflict of ideas from personal conflict is partly a matter of intent. It is also a function of language. Keep the language of discussion attached to the idea, not the people. Personalized language—"Your idea won't work because . . . "—comes across as rejection of the person as well as rejection of the idea and fosters defensive reaction.

It's difficult to separate idea conflict, as in "the idea won't work," from personal conflict when the conflict occurs between different levels in a hierarchy. Fearful of losing reputation or position, subordinates tend to stifle their disagreement with a superior, and while this practice promotes consensus decision making, it kills creative exploration. Senior managers who are sensitive to it can learn how to encourage vigorous subordinate participation in productive conflict.

Conrad Paulus, a manager of product development at AT&T, managed to keep everyone productively involved through conflict at a time when one of his developers

got excited about a product idea we called the "Any-Hour Saver Calling Plan." The higher-ups blew the developer's idea apart, but she didn't want to let it go. She and I came into the office on a Saturday and argued about the concept all day. I assumed the advocacy for the company, and each of us tried to prove the other wrong. The day's work resulted in a perspective neither of us had thought about before. I went with her to take the improved idea back to the company, and this time it was accepted. The kind of arguing we did that day works only if both sides can feel unthreatened and are willing to change if necessary.[6]

Maureen Arkle, a vice president at Tufts Health Care Plan, explains how Tufts builds self-standing teams—accountable for results but independent in thought and action—to deal with the challenges of hierarchy:

We are very careful about how we get these teams going. If someone at a higher level states something too strongly, people feel they shouldn't disagree. They'll be silent or just go along, and we lose the potential richness of their contributions. Our model is to take a cross-section of people, say, "Here's the situation; we need a solution," and then let them work on it any way they want. We don't micromanage. We generally give people a direction and a blank slate. They don't need to come back for permission, and they can implement the results as they see fit. This gives the team power and confidence to come up with the best solution they can.[7]

Encourage Risk Taking

Companies that encourage risk taking increase the likelihood that their employees will in fact take the risk of breaking and making connections and so accomplish the critical work of the creative process. Paradoxically, and fortunately, the short-term risk involved in challenging assumptions and breaking connections reduces the longer-term and more dangerous risk of relying on outdated assumptions. When employees risk challenging whatever might be a company's sacred assumption, they take the blinders off the company's perception of its world. And if the sacred assumption turns out to be flawed, the employees are in a position to generate new ideas that will redirect the company before it gets into serious trouble. The point is that if you shut down what seems to be high-risk creative problem solving, if you get cold feet while challenging familiar assumptions and developing alternative courses of action, you inadvertently shut down risk taking at a point when actual risk is not only low but also necessary for long-term survival.

Sophisticated risk-assessment models can be very helpful at the decision point for implementation of significant solutions. Care needs to be taken that they are not used either too early or to screen out creative experiments that, while risky from a predictability point of view, don't threaten the enterprise.

Any action holds the risk of uncertain results. No action at all holds the risk of death from entropy. Risk is a fact of life. To embrace risk in the early stages of the creative process, specifically in the breaking and making of connections, is to manage risk in the most productive way.

Individual tolerances for risk and for different types of risk vary. Some members of a team involved in innovation may feel comfortable deferring answers and solutions, letting themselves remain open and fluid until most of the pieces fall into place. Other members may become increasingly anxious and exert pressure to reach a decision. It takes only a few comments like "Nobody's ever done that before" and "The boss will hate it" and "Come on, get to the point" to spread anxiety through a group and build a groundswell of opposition to experimental thinking and support for ideas that have worked before.

Often, the pressure of time and the risk of wasting it triggers this sort of anxiety and drives managers to prematurely shut down a creative effort. Breaking old connections and making new ones takes time; accepting the risk and allowing the time matter enormously in executing the dynamic successfully to carry through effectively in the rest of the creative process to useful ideas.

Compromises in favor of fast decisions and safe answers occur most frequently in large hierarchies and highly competitive environments where taking the time to think reflectively or creatively can be seen as the biggest risk of all. Heiko Lotz, the divisional bank director whose strategic forecasting we discussed in chapters 1 and 2, has had difficulty even broaching an undirected conversation with colleagues about their business. "We have to force ourselves to take the time to sit in a room for a day or two to explore alternate possibilities for the future." It's Lotz's mandate to insist that his colleagues take the lesser risk of spending time on strategic reflection.

Despite the need to allow a full measure of time for the best connections, the best connections can occasionally be made and the right idea generated quickly. In the situation where bureaucratic delay is likely to thwart implementation, acting quickly can be appropriate for breaking and making connections and carrying the creative process through to executing a necessary idea.

Mary McKenney, while employed by a New York bank, said, "Sometimes dealing with the bureaucracy and waiting for approvals is the real danger." McKenney's former boss pulled off a successful creative response to a fast-moving situation that would have failed if left to the normal approval process:

> *Investment products were the linchpin in our Treasury solutions, tying together disbursement and collection services. Offering a variety of tax-advantaged, high-return products was critical to being able to attract deposits, which led naturally to our ability to sell our payment products. Some of our competitors were offering investment products with higher interest rates and better features. Our in-house group could not respond in a timely fashion with new product development. A colleague of mine did the research necessary to identify a set of third-party investment products that would competitively advantage us in the marketplace and made the proposal that those products be included in our solutions. This was a politically charged proposal, since our own investment products would be competing directly with products that we would be offering, and it offended some of our in-house product managers. I was prepared for a delay or no decision but was pleasantly surprised when my boss immediately approved the idea, in spite of the political threats. We put the whole offer together in six weeks and ended up increasing revenue to our Treasury business by*

over 200 percent within six months. We grew business with existing customers, who now found it appealing to buy collection and payment products from our bank because we could offer them attractive investment returns on their deposits, and we bought ourselves the time to develop our own new products by using a competitor's advantage creatively. It was a real win-win for everyone.[8]

However, time may also work to discourage the risk of breaking established connections and making useful new ones. Creativity depends on embracing the risk.

Periodically, even in companies that recognize the virtue of risk, threats to risk taking arise from the pressure of larger market circumstances. A company must try to counter these threats as assiduously as it resists the more usual anxieties of time. According to Jorge Bermudez, executive vice president of Citibank's e-business, in the early 1990s "Citibank got into a difficult financial situation and risk taking dropped; as a result innovation dropped. But we knew we had to stay creative. If we became commoditized and competed on the basis of price, we'd become obsolete."[9] In this case, the company countered the threat to risk taking by both calculating and spreading the risk.

Sam Borenstein, head of innovation for Citibank's e-business, says that the bank has now been decentralized so that no one locus of decision making can "affect the whole" enough to cause irreparable damage. He also says that the bank has been using mathematical models to better understand and predict the risk associated with creative projects. These changes provide a margin of safety on one hand and on the other hand allow individual divisions to more freely encourage risk.[10]

Promote Diversity

Diversity brings breadth of perspective to the tasks of identifying and criticizing age-old assumptions and recognizing new possibility. The founders of Synectics considered diversity of thinking so important that they composed the company name from ancient Greek words meaning the "bringing together of diverse elements."

Selecting for Diversity in Groups

When groups are purposefully constructed to include diverse perspectives, the groups gain in terms of the number and variety of angles from which a problem can be assessed. The productive conflict in the groups will have a range and richness that enhance the ideas the group generates.

One Web-oriented design firm in Boston makes sure that representatives of its creative, technology, and strategy departments take part in every decision. The firm knows that each of these functions uses different criteria and believes that taking all of the criteria into account will produce a better product.

Universal Studios goes even deeper, discriminating among types of creative thinking and requiring that people of each type participate in every project. As Phil Hettema, a former vice president, explains:

> There are three types of creative thinkers. There are the good idea people, who look at a problem and return with a solution. There are the reflective people, who see connections and understand how work on problem one can apply to problem two. And there are the people who can conceptualize entire systems and worlds in their head. Here we need all three types to turn out good productions.[11]

People with diverse expertise can also be assembled on an ad hoc basis for a single project. One bank sometimes brought technical staff together with product managers and marketing specialists to create new products. On one occasion, this assemblage of diverse staff, working with supercomputers, not only delivered the new products but came up with a new way to form and reform global partnerships around breaking opportunities. This team also prompted the establishment of a task force for another area for development, a deeper trial relationship with a major auto manufacturer whereby both the bank and the manufacturer were able to analyze all finances, enabling the bank to be a better advisory partner. The only permanent members of the effort were the product managers; everyone else added their expertise and perspective to the process of invention, then left.

Fostering Diverse Intelligence

To staff diverse groups, a company must have a diversity of employees and of types of thinking. Many companies lack this diversity.

Howard Gardner, director of Harvard University's Project Zero for the study of human potential, theorizes that there are eight basic types of intelligence but that only two—the linguistic and the logical/mathematical—are honored in schools or in business.[12] As a result, some companies that acknowledge this lack of diversity recruit people like poet David Whyte, conductor and musician Ben Zander, and many visual artists for their ability to stimulate different senses, fresh perspectives on old assumptions, or new ideas altogether.

One Web consulting company employs full-time staff artists in all phases of its business. The creative director of the company comments, "We hire a lot of people with fine arts backgrounds. Art teaches you how to look and how to derive meaning from what you are looking at. You can see a tree from nine different perspectives. That type of vision translates directly back into business. It gives you the ability to see beyond what is to what could be."

Roger Schank, director of Northwestern University's Institute for the Learning Sciences, also laments the educational system. "To do well in this tradition-bound [educational] environment, you don't need to be smart; you need to be a grind. Breaking the rules is how you get smarter, and this is frowned upon by educators."[13]

Although education is now beginning to address the criticism from Gardner and Schank, for many people in corporate America today the damage has been done. For most of these people, work-place training can be a solution. Training that enables today's business people to challenge established knowledge, to welcome new ideas tolerantly, to think about their own thinking, is a boon. At Frito-Lay, employees who were trained in creativity produced ideas that led to $100 million in cost reductions over four years.[14] At Sysco, employees who participated in creativity training increased their sales by an average of 25 percent to 30 percent.[15]

Some companies offer creativity training programs broadly to all employees, while others focus on particular task groups. Each time Lucien Frohling, a director at Citibank, moved into a new position, he sent his new staff off site for creative problem-solving training because "it always helps the group work together more fluidly and effectively."[16] Pat Wnek of James River Manufacturing found creativity seminars made his engineers more willing to risk offering "half-baked ideas," many of which turned out to be worth researching and developing.[17]

Diversity at the Leadership Level

Without diversity of thinking and perspective in its leaders, a company is less likely to identify creative employees, less likely to embrace the conflict inherent in breaking and making connections, and quite likely to lack the range of vision needed to make the best use of whatever creativity it is able to stimulate. Yet leadership is naturally often the least diverse group in a company. Using the Myers-Briggs profile—a personality model that types people based on how they process information, make decisions, direct their energy, and organize their lives—Steve Leichtman studied the senior leaders at Tufts Health Care Plan. He found that they were predominantly

sensing, judging types, types that are very often found among senior management. We had only a few temperaments that match inventors, and no adventurer types. Our leadership culture tended to make those with preferences other than the norm a bit uncomfortable. We've addressed that now. Over the past several years, the executives we've brought onto our leadership team have helped to broaden and balance our perspective. As a result, our leadership group's ability to think creatively has been greatly enhanced.[18]

Diversity also surfaced as a concern for leaders of a U.S. strategy consulting firm. In a creativity training program, the leaders were discussing the barriers to creative thinking at the corporate level when one of the leaders remarked, "We promote people who act like us." There was silence as this comment sank in. The six senior members of the company, who had started the company, were entrepreneurs and risk takers, but much like one another in many ways. They had unconsciously built a company in which everyone else had backgrounds like theirs and behaved as they did. So the company lacked the diversity that gives richness and range to connection breaking and making.

The next level down in this consulting company consisted of very smart people who, observing the behaviors of those high in position and authority, emphasized those behaviors in themselves at the expense of individual expression. Thus the leaders inadvertently reinforced this sameness by promoting people whose talents, ideas, and opinions were familiar and comfortable to them.

The leaders pursued the creativity training because, as one founder noted, "It's gotten very boring here. If we don't take chances in house, how can we recommend anything really new to our clients?" The tendency toward sameness, which many leadership teams unknowingly exhibit, puts a company in danger of tunnel vision right where an organization can least afford it—at the top.

It's worth noting that diversity can also present dangers. When diversity at the leadership level comes without a deep, shared understanding of a company's fundamental purpose and values, it slows decisions and weakens collaboration.

Diversity committed to serving the company will result in creative, functional harmony.

Organize for Intrinsic Motivation

Groups, like individuals, perform more creatively when intrinsically motivated. Here we consider how to organize groups specifically to harness the virtues of intrinsic motivation.

Coalitions

When people voluntarily organize themselves to solve a problem or realize a new idea, they are making what we call a coalition. In a coalition, each member brings his or her unique energy, enthusiasm, and creativity to the task. Participating in its formation, pursuing its goal not because of assignment but from their own volition, members of a coalition possess a degree of intrinsic motivation that's rarely matched, along with the freedom to challenge assumptions, that can provide the commitment necessary to create bold new connections.

Because of their voluntary and often ad hoc stature, coalitions may initially lack resources or authority. But the virtues of a coalition usually outweigh this drawback. Coalition reporting relationships and structures can shift flexibly with circumstances and allow members to contribute freely wherever talents and inclinations are strongest. And self-determining, intrinsic motivation sustains members through setbacks on the road to generating and selecting and implementing the right ideas.

Mary Sonnack, director for new product development at 3M, pieced together a coalition after becoming excited about research being done by Dr. Erik von Hippel at MIT. Von Hippel had found that working with what he termed "lead users"—people who have advanced knowledge and experience that only others in the particular niche share—could increase both the number and the success of new product ideas. Sonnack enlisted von Hippel's support and then asked managers and scientists at 3M to participate in exploring the lead user phenomenon. Initially, she had no authority to put together a formal initiative, but the 15 percent personal research time allowed by 3M let her and others who were interested explore a potentially fruitful avenue that was not part of official corporate endeavor.[19]

Surgical draping is the fabric, often paper, taped to the skin around an incision during surgery to keep the incision antiseptic. Scientists and managers in 3M's surgical drape business felt a need for new product ideas and sensed a possibility for new ideas in the lead user concept. They joined Sonnack's coalition, and in the investigative stage of the initiative, looking for needs relevant to their product line, visited medical clinics in several developing countries.

At one clinic, the members of the coalition noticed that physicians were not using any modern surgical draping materials. When asked why, the doctors replied that the clinic could not afford them. Resulting infections in patients or staff were treated with antibiotic drugs, which were cheap but lost effectiveness as bacteria became resistant to them.

The coalition decided to look for techniques for producing dramatically less expensive antiseptic surgical draping that developing countries would be able to afford. In the spirit of von Hippel's research, the team started searching in what might be innovative niches for people who were already dealing with different aspects of this problem. They looked at veterinary hospitals, where costs not only had to be kept low but where conditions and patients were not antiseptic. How veterinary surgeons were keeping their incisions antiseptic and inexpensive would not necessarily have filtered out to the medical profession, so the vets might in fact prove to be lead users in the context of the needs of developing countries. The coalition also talked to professional makeup artists, who needed to temporarily but frequently stick various materials to their clients' skin without causing irritation and infection. Here again were potential lead users, people working in a niche who might provide a solution to a problem outside their niche.

As it happened, both the vets and the makeup artists did prove to be lead users in the context of surgical draping. Both had jury-rigged solutions to their particular needs in exposing flesh to infection and preventing infection. Working directly with the lead users, adapting their jury-rigged solutions, Sonnack's coalition constructed an array of new, workable, and inexpensive surgical draping materials for medicine in developing countries. "We have eight divisions doing this kind of lead user research now," Sonnack says.

While the lead user concept bears noting for its success here, the informal nature of the original coalition Sonnack formed is in part responsible for the method's success. As Sonnack says, "Very creative people don't always work well in organized teams. They see teams as a waste of time, and they see the movement to form teams as a fad. They're wary of losing their individual creativity." Intrinsic motivation drives what we call coalitions and usually drives them to successful results.

Teams

Companies often form teams when they want to tackle problems or search out opportunities. Resources are assigned, reporting procedures established, team members chosen for their strengths and availability. Each person has a role and works toward the project goal. And there's efficiency in all this. But formalized relationships can hamper flexibility; poor fits in talent or style may be hard to correct, and members directed to participate may join without deep intrinsic motivation—both of which sap creativity.

Adapting the traits of successful coalitions, however, will ameliorate some of the natural drawbacks of an assigned team. First, involve each team member from the outset in the establishment of goals and determination of procedure to invest each member in the team's success. As individuals feel ownership for the team's work and their place in that work, their personal commitment increases. Second, give teams time for members to sort out the best ways to work together. Taking this time may compromise speed and accountability at first, but once members have agreed among themselves on goals, deadlines, and roles, the team will operate as a much stronger, more efficient unit. Individual members often find it particularly important to control how they allocate their time between work on the team and other duties.

Rowers in crew racing talk about the magic of the "set-up," the moment when all the rowers in a boat suddenly seem to operate as one. No one can make it happen, but it does happen most often when each member wants to be on the crew, shares a common goal and degree of desire, and has had time to practice with crewmates. Companies that form their teams with the same care and attention will give these teams a healthy balance of intrinsic as well as extrinsic motivation, and the teams will have a good chance at matching the peak connection breaking and making performance of coalitions.

Information Flows
That Support Creativity

The final key to breaking and making connections serves as lubricant and context for every other key. Conflict, risk taking, diversity, and organizing for intrinsic motivation all ultimately depend on the flow of information.

Creatively healthy companies have a high volume of diverse information that flows freely throughout the organization, increasing the likelihood of collision among beliefs, presumptions, possibilities, and new facts. These sorts of collisions can lead to the breaking and making of connections and the creation of new ideas.

Technology continues to compound the amount of information available that you have to manage, so you may, understandably, resist still more information. In fact, we are not encouraging more. Our principal message here is not to pour on more data but to consider the availability, diversity, and flow of information. Productive creativity requires depth of information in the relevant domain as well as information about related spheres of knowledge. This information already exists in many companies.

But we also advocate exposure to information from apparently irrelevant sources, including the arts. This information doesn't require day-to-day management. It serves as a catalyst to breaking and making connections within the pool of information already at your disposal. The freedom with which information passes through a working group—and the willingness to infuse catalysts into the information to promote collisions among beliefs and presumptions and facts—determines whether and how old assumptions will break down and new connections lead to new ideas.

Using More and Less Information

An oil company was looking for new ways of dealing with mixed-fluid reservoirs, deposits of mixed oil and water that impose the extra costs of bringing the mix to the surface, then separating the oil from the water, and finally putting the water back in the ground. One member of the group of engineers studying the problem wondered about separating the water and oil underground so that only oil would be pumped to the surface. Underground separation had been tried before without success, and this group had not considered trying it again. But the group had not come up with any better approach to their problem, so they gathered chemists, physicists, and engineers from inside and outside the petroleum industry—an extraordinarily diverse set of experts turned loose on the question of mixed-well reservoirs. The collective expertise broke down enough constraining assumptions and then made enough useful connections to develop more than a dozen potentially fruitful experiments in underground separation.

The members of the original group of engineers did not themselves have all the information they needed, but they understood that the information existed, so they added it to their own resources. The information from a wide variety of knowledge bases, when brought to focus on this single problem, produced the ideal connection-breaking and -making vehicle.

In the right circumstances, supplementing information in a problem area with a great deal more information—diverse information, related, but not the existing information—can powerfully serve creativity. By contrast, in other circumstances, distilling and manipulating information readily at hand, information that is acknowledged to define the problem, can lead to the breaking and making of connections that will successfully resolve the problem.

A consultant, asked to help a food company create unique entries for a long-established, slow-changing category of products, gathered ample but predictably relevant information from researchers and consumer groups. The consultant and a small core group from the food company broke this information down into hundreds of discrete data points, and then the group discussed, dissected, created metaphors, analogies, and possible story lines, and recombined the data until the points naturally coalesced into thirteen fundamental insights about consumer eating behavior, some of which were particularly fresh and promising. A larger group from the food company then focused on the these few insights and developed forty entirely new food concepts for a category that most people in the company thought had run its course.

In this case the usual amount and scope of information was sufficient. What was necessary for new connections to new food concepts was for the creative groups to see the information in a new light and from different angles. Thus the constricting assumptions and new possibilities within the information became apparent.

Added information and manipulation of existing information can help break and make connections. An absence of information can also help. When Edwin Land's three-year-old daughter asked him why she couldn't see a photograph right after it was taken, he took her question seriously.[20] He looked for ways to connect her idea with his understanding of chemistry, and thus he invented the Polaroid instant photographic process. If Land's daughter had had even a cursory understanding of photography, much less known anything about the chemistry of photography, she might not have even imagined her connection-breaking question. This vignette speaks to the worth of occasionally getting entirely outside a sphere of endeavor and its weight of information to look back at the problem with ignorant or naïve curiosity.

Unrelated Information

Unrelated information can contribute powerfully to breaking and making connections. The cockleburs that George de Mestral found stuck to his clothes and his dog after a walk in the woods led him to envision a fastening system that became Velcro.[21] In fable, the falling apple crystallized Newton's thinking about gravity.

Unrelated information automatically distracts creative problem solvers from relevant information that sometimes presses too close to be recognizably useful in any new way. Surprisingly often, distraction and the unrelated information it heralds will spark a breakdown of preconceptions in the relevant information and provide the new insight that leads to new ideas.

Creative companies take advantage of this phenomenon by disseminating unrelated corporate information randomly or purposefully through formal or informal channels. 3M, for example, requires all technologies and applications of technology to be shared on the company's global Web-based communication system. Employees can of course use this pool of information to access material directly relevant to their work. But they can also browse for news of work by creative minds at the far reaches of the company. In this unrelated information, researchers can and frequently do find the catalyst for new ideas in their own quite separate work.

Universal Studios achieves a similar stimulus with a less formal method, as Phil Hettema, former vice president for attraction development, explains. "A few of our leaders are continually in touch with everything going on both within and beyond individual project groups. They move easily in and out of project teams, adding new ideas in one place, removing ideas from another place, and channeling other ideas where they are needed."

Many companies, aware of the tendency of bureaucracy to create functional silos, make it a point to build in communication links between potential silos so that unrelated information will have dedicated channels through which to circulate. A few creatively astute organizations design work environments that physically encourage the exchange of unrelated information. Architect Gunter Henn designed the Technical University in Munich so that departments representing all academic disciplines encircle a single plaza that contains restaurants and meeting areas. As a result, people who would normally not meet bump up against one another and have the chance to share seemingly unrelated information in the natural course of every workday. Dr. Henn designed a Volkswagen automobile manufacturing plant in Germany along the same lines, putting the administrative offices between the assembly lines, forcing increased informal interaction between the various functions of the plant.[22]

If you want to use unrelated information in a directed way for a specific problem, you can do so. Direct a flow of unrelated information toward your problem area. If you select the information with an eye as to how and how much it is unrelated, to some extent you focus the direction the results will take.

When executives at Citibank gathered to develop new ideas for transferring currency across borders, they first investigated more or less unrelated trends in society and technology. At the time, data mining, intelligent agents, and artificial intelligence techniques were just coming out of laboratories, and the business trends of outsourcing, mass customization, and globalization of business had been predicted but were not yet a reality. The executives in Citibank's working group were presented with research to loosen their minds and broaden their range of thinking. The group subsequently came up with new, almost instant, methods by which the bank could account for and build funding strategies among multiple borders and currencies. The group also generated new methods for predicting success in prospective foreign investment and development, methods that would not have emerged without the stimulation provided by the unrelated information the group received.

To this point, we've discussed the flow of information later-ally and down through the company. The flow up, to company leaders, is just as important. In this spirit, Bill Gates used to read every e-mail message sent to him by Microsoft employees because the messages challenged his thinking. And he responded to most of the messages to keep the exchanges—and arguments—going.[23] Once or twice a year Gates goes off on an isolated retreat. These are his "think weeks," where he reads articles often unrelated to current Microsoft affairs to stimulate his thinking on the next critical issues for Microsoft.[24]

As a group leader at an international pharmaceutical firm, Peter Carlin created the position of an ombudsman to whom em-ployees could safely bring any ideas at all—including complaints. The ombudsman would in turn deliver the ideas anonymously to Carlin. The system opened a direct channel to Carlin for views that were often entirely unrelated to what was on his mind. This increased the chances of Carlin's own views being challenged in a way they might not otherwise have been. He didn't agree with everything he heard, but he was convinced that the division was stronger for the range of perspectives he had to consider.[25]

New Thinking from Outside

Most new thinking occurs outside any given company, and sometimes new thinking determines the shape of emerging infor-mation that will shatter the assumptions on which the given com-pany and others like it are built. Companies that keep on top of new thinking will be able to anticipate challenges to their business and understand emerging information not as a threat but as a chance for new ideas and competitive advantage.

Heiko Lotz regularly engages an organization consulting in global political and economic trends to help managers at his bank spot trends in new thinking as they imagine potential sce-narios for the bank. Simple focus groups can also keep your hand on the pulse of some important types of new thinking. To be ready with new ideas for products of its own, accounting firm

KPMG interviews groups of clients and potential clients about their needs and fears.[26] The Jim Beam Company creates new drink ideas (and avoids being stuck with old ones) by bringing together bartenders and bar owners whose expertise in the habits of young adults is more timely and accurate than any number of demographic studies.[27]

As a way of staying on top of new thinking, Microsoft rigorously uses customer feedback. Michael Cusumano, a professor of strategy at MIT's Sloan School of Management, believes that Microsoft analyzes its feedback and channels the information into product development more quickly, systematically, and thoroughly than any other company in the United States, with the result that the company can often better anticipate market turns.[28] And to keep up with new thinking that has global reverberations, many companies align themselves with academic and research institutions or professional associations.

Organizational Structures to Enhance Information Flow

The structure of a company can unwittingly strangle the information flow needed to break and make connections. In large, hierarchical organizations, employees get caught between the functions to the left and right of them, their boss's level of authority over them, and their subordinates below. As a result, the information they generate doesn't easily get out to where it might be of service, and they do not always receive the information they themselves could use.

In contrast, many entrepreneurial companies with small or no hierarchies and loose structures form and reform around changing markets and capital, watching for opportunities in their shifting environments. Information in these companies is usually more open, readily accessible, and shared freely between individuals who formulate the organization's aims.

Like loose entrepreneurial governance, organized job rotation and matrix organization are attempts at corporate structures that liberate and circulate information, that foster the making and breaking of connections and, in doing so, foster the creative process.

Job rotation is a well-known solution to the problem of circulating information through large companies. At Citibank, top executives must rotate through a number of departments, functions, and even countries before they become eligible for promotion to the next level. Each rotation enriches the thinking of both the individual and the department, and it helps prevent the calcification of assumptions. Ad hoc or informal job rotations accomplish the same thing. In one senior executive's department at a large pharmaceutical company, every manager spends one day a month at a field office making sales calls, staying in touch with local problems and opportunities, picking up direct front-line information about customer needs. In a matrix, individual staff members at least as far down as middle management may have one role that's functional, such as sales or marketing, and another role of a different sort, such as management over a particular product or team. This increases the range and nature of information employees encounter on a regular basis. A potential additional benefit to creativity is that, because employees report to two or more entirely different parts of the hierarchy, they make some of their own decisions about allocating their time among their various responsibilities. In an environment that fosters high responsibility and independent movement across vertical lines of command, traditional authority shrinks and, as Harvard Business School professor Rosabeth Moss Kanter says, "influence must substitute for authority."[29] This kind of situation powerfully enhances intrinsic motivation, making the crosscurrents of information even more likely to stimulate connection breaking and making.

Matrix organizations can take as long as three to five years to reach peak function, in part because the increased communication introduces a high level of complexity to negotiations around decision making.[30] But once made, decisions are often implemented faster because there is more knowledge, focus, and commitment among the various stakeholders. A poorly implemented matrix can be bogged down by ambiguity and unbalanced authority, but Kanter's research found that, on the whole, a matrix produces more innovation precisely because it increases information, perspectives, resources, freedom, and complexity in relationships.

At matrix-organized MRW, a communications firm in Boston, Rebekah Kaufman is director of business development and also oversees the company's interns and their professional development. The way she performs her two roles, as she reports it, "is to move between both several times a day. When one gets frustrating, I switch to the other for a while." She finds that in each role she interacts with a different set of people, widening her contacts, increasing the diversity of information she's exposed to, and improving her opportunities to share and benefit from a range of ideas and information. She has seen the information she disseminates, as well as information she receives, rupture constraining assumptions and generate useful new ideas. She herself has used this creative opportunity to increase the company's new business substantially and to mentor the generation of staff that handles it.

———

Creativity remains a process in which each of the four dynamics—motivation, curiosity, breaking and making connections, and evaluation—has a critical place. Breaking and making connections is the dynamic at the heart of creativity, the kinetic violence of change that gives creativity such revolutionary potential—the potential to turn the dismay of a threatened old-line company like Steelcase into an exciting new business model.

Because of its importance in the process, breaking and making connections demands singular attention. If you want to be creative, you want above all to challenge assumptions and break connections; and you want to make the new connections that generate new ideas. This is the creative action.

Part Two

Climate

FOUR

The Climate for Creativity in an Enterprise

IN CHAPTER 3, we looked at breaking and making connections and at the keys to successfully engaging that critical dynamic. Climate is the key to engaging the other three dynamics of the creative process, motivation, curiosity and fear, and evaluation.

Expectations and Behavior Underpin Climate

Each time you interact with others, you contribute to a mutual environment that influences the expectations and behavior of everyone in the environment, whether two people, a team, an office, or an entire company. Each person in a given environment tends, consciously or unconsciously, to act in ways that reinforce other people's expectations. Reinforcing others' expectations gives back a sense of belonging and safety; it also increases the ability to influence others to behave one way or another.

Based on what they feel is needed to survive and succeed, people behave differently—perhaps confidently, perhaps timidly or aggressively. They might move from cautious behavior with superiors and joking with colleagues to professional warmth with customers and genuine animation with children. In turn, the superiors, colleagues, customers, and kids respond in kind.

People simultaneously read all the expectations and behaviors in an environment, form expectations of their own, and behave accordingly. Each person in the environment experiences the environment uniquely—and most often without seeing his or her own part in it. The common collection of behaviors and expectations makes what we call a climate.

Business literature often uses climate and culture interchangeably. In this book, we make a distinction. Climate, as we speak of it, is *part* of a company's culture. A company's culture also includes its heritage and embedded structures, technology, patterns of communication, and so on.[1] Climate influences and is influenced by the other cultural elements, but it is nonetheless distinct from them and from culture. In a few of the examples below, people use the word "culture" when referring to what we call climate; we note the discrepancy.

Climate Stability

People often behave in ways that meet expectations. And people form expectations from the behaviors they observe. As a result, climates tend toward equilibrium and tend to stay in equilibrium until patterns of both expectation and behavior change. For example, if a colleague has offered to support an employee's project several times and each time has not come through with the support, the employee will not expect support to materialize if it is offered again. Expectations do not change if behavior does not change. Expectations change only after behavior changes.

On the other side of the equation, behavior—what people do and say—does not change much if expectations don't change. Students are likely to behave and perform to teacher expectations regardless of whether the teacher tries to hide the expectations or even holds them unconsciously.[2] When people expect to meet hostility, they frequently behave anxiously, defensively, or belligerently even before encountering the hostility.

Memory plays a role in climate. Expectations change if behavior changes, but it doesn't happen right away. If a superior reneges on a promise, an employee will listen more skeptically to promises in the future. If the same superior acts on a promise in the future, the situation isn't likely to turn around immediately; gaining the confidence and changing the expectations of the employee will take repeatedly fulfilled promises. Similarly, past supportive behavior by a superior will sustain an employee's expectations of fidelity even if momentary pressures distract the superior from a commitment. Memory serves as a delaying sea anchor that keeps climate equilibrium in place against day-to-day tides and currents of change.

Global and Local Climates

The larger the group, the more powerful and stable the climate around that group. Most companies are started by just a few leaders or a single entrepreneur. When the founders hire new people, they select candidates who meet their expectations for skills and character, for desired behavior now and in the future. The applicants themselves form opinions about what to expect at the organization. Their initial expectations adjust over time to match the prevailing climate of interlocking behaviors and expectations. They learn which behaviors earn approval, which warrant censure, which get things done. Before long, the applicants become part of the climate, adding to the climate's stability.

Long-term climates give vivid character to whole companies, allowing even people outside a company to form expectations about what it's like inside the company. One expects, for instance, to encounter a different climate or atmosphere at Universal Studios than at IBM. But within the overall climate of an entire company there will also be local climates through which people pass regularly. An employee at Universal Studios may work a riotous lunch with comedy writers, then attend a serious scheduling conference, and later give a presentation to an intimidating committee.

Unique climates can also form within different functional and professional groups of a company. A vice president of marketing may expect analytical rigor from a finance department and independent thinking from a researcher. The expectations may be mistaken, but they will nevertheless influence the marketing executive's behavior.

Local climates give their clues, spoken (rarely) and unspoken (usually), about what one should expect and how to behave. No one person guides or purposefully shapes mutual expectations and behaviors. Local climates and the larger climates that contain them or radiate from them most often develop by default as patterns of behavior and expectation continue to reinforce each other over time.

Climates for Creativity

Climates conducive to creativity nurture the individuality at the heart of intrinsic motivation. They provide the safety necessary for curiosity to flourish. They provide support and patience for successful evaluation. They expect newness.

To put this sort of climate in place in a large company with complexities of structure, varieties of people, and a weight of institutional memory takes prolonged effort. Companies often begin such effort on a limited scale, experimenting to determine exactly which creative expectations and behaviors to encourage and how to encourage them. In the three stories that follow, individual leaders used different tactics to make three distinct creative climates. The tactics in each case and the resulting climates suited the needs of each company.

Building Internal Boundaries to Nurture Creative Talent

When David Welty became corporate creative director of Hallmark's Specialty Creative Division in 1994, he faced a formidable challenge. "From the 1940s to the 1980s life at Hallmark was good," says Welty. "We were profitable, and our richness allowed an experimental climate. Creativity just came out naturally." But as the greeting card industry became more competitive, everything changed. "The increased pressure was motivating for some of our creative people and demotivating for others," Welty says. "I needed to build a creative climate inside a results-driven business culture that would nurture a wide range of creative types."[3]

Welty's first initiative was to wall off the Specialty Creative Division from the rest of the corporate culture by convincing corporate leaders to allow the division autonomy in its design process. To ensure that this autonomy did not threaten corporate priorities, he included managers from outside the division in the process of evaluating concepts. "We decided that everything would be evaluated first by us in creative, second by the customer, then by management," which "reassured the business side enough that they felt less need to control us."

Building this barrier between his group and the rest of the organization allowed Welty the freedom he wanted to form a climate that differed from Hallmark's prevailing environment at the time. He then hired midlevel managers who could help create the supportive environment he envisioned. Midlevel managers were central to Welty's strategy because the quality of relationship between managers and direct reports is critical to staff morale and the subjective aspects of intrinsic motivation. Midlevel managers "are the key enablers," he explains. "They can help motivate or demotivate people. They know how to form the

right team for each job. The best managers are like orchestra con-
ductors: They know their instruments, or people, and play each
according to their strengths for each performance. They know
that now it is time to bring up the brass, now to lower the sound
and hear the violins."

Finding that kind of manager was a challenge. Before Welty
inherited the department, its diversity had declined, resulting in a
diminished range of artistic sensibilities and weak management.
Welty promoted from within, putting artists rather than professional managers into critical managerial positions. "Promoting
our own people gives us leaders—the midlevel managers—who
understand Hallmark, creativity, and our people." In his hiring,
Welty evaluated potential staff for his department according to
sixteen personality types. "When I came in, we had only intro-
verted artistic types in the group. Now I try to have all sixteen
personality styles in the division and a good distribution of them
on each team." The spread of styles this distribution has produced is great enough and the types of work in the division broad
enough to make it possible for every individual to find his or
her own variety of challenge, while the department as a whole
demonstrates wide artistic range consistent with good business.

Once his staffing was in place, Welty addressed the balance
of productive and fallow time that he had learned was essential
to the artists' productivity. He allocated 30 percent of the division's time and resources to "recharging the artistic talent of our
people . . . freshening the mind with experiences that can be purposefully drawn on in later work." Employees could take paid
sabbaticals to pursue relevant interests. Research trips became
common. "We'll pay for trips to Vienna to study the masters and
soak in the atmosphere," says Welty. Closer to home, Hallmark
operates a creative retreat center on a farm that any employee can
visit and that offers classes to augment or hone the tools of artistic expression. The company also maintains a rotating art collection and a library with magazines from around the world.

Welty segregated his division to protect it from the rough-
and-tumble of Hallmark's larger climate. Then he fashioned a

local climate to support, diversify, and sustain the brand of creative talent Hallmark traded on.

A Creative Climate Based on Principles

Pete Karolczak had an opportunity to build a creative division from the ground up when he was tapped by Hewlett-Packard to form a new software venture. As he assessed the requirements of the intended group, he knew that the group "would be under pressure to deliver software solutions quickly. We would have to stay creative and flexible. And we would need expertise that spanned many departments."[4]

Karolczak knew that these goals also required avoiding a silo orientation. He wanted the cross-functional information flow and the multifunctional coalition building that generate and implement new ideas, so he could not afford a confining organizational structure. Referring to culture (but in fact speaking about what we call climate), Karolczak says, "I sat there on the first day and thought, 'Do I build an organization or a culture?' I decided to develop a culture that matched the creativity we needed to accomplish, then hire into it."

Karolczak based his new group's climate on three fundamental principles; everything else had to support them or at least not undermine them. The first principle was collaboration. "For creativity to flourish," Karolczak explains, "you need multiple perspectives." Diverse perspectives strengthen creative outcomes, but since people would be coming together for the first time from distinct functions with quite divergent expertise, the people he hired needed to be willing and able to accommodate the attendant conflict and still feel safe enough to engage their curiosity and share information and work collaboratively.

The second principle was open feedback so that everyone would know what was going on and where they stood. Karolczak established a 360-degree review process, making each person accountable to every other person in the team. Very quickly, the 360-degree review became daily standard operating procedure.

The frequent feedback kept people on track with project goals. Among people with a high degree of intrinsic motivation, the review reinforced that motivation and at the same time provided a steadying measure of extrinsic motivation.

The third principle was flexibility: "In a business like ours every half-year is different. We always have to be open to changing ourselves." To increase flexibility, he abandoned Hewlett-Packard's standard cubicle environment to set up common work spaces. Four- to eight-person teams were arranged in a circle, backs to the center, so that people could talk easily with their team and pass by other groupings to shoot the breeze about the latest user interface or last night's game. As Karolczak explained it, "To create collective knowledge, we need this kind of spontaneous information sharing. Conversations start up all the time, people chiming in and out whenever they want." Each team member also had a small personal space they could use when they needed privacy. And for hanging out or special meetings, team rooms were furnished with comfortable chairs and sofas. This sort of flexibility encourages intrinsic motivation and the play of curiosity.

Altogether, Karolczak said, "We spent much more time the first year tending to process—the social aspects of communication, our philosophy, and how we worked together—and let the business plan run its course without too much adjustment. We developed a certain kind of environment that worked well for us, and we never had to institute a lot of measurements and controls."

Karolczak's principles of collaboration, feedback, and flexibility shaped a functioning creative climate. And, as he hoped, speed, productivity, and quality were a byproduct of the climate; the unit has grown to 250 people and continues to deliver good software on time. Karolczak planned to start other units based on the same principles, building a larger division around freestanding units of a few hundred people each.

Building a Creative Climate in a New Company

Research has shown that creative groups brought into a larger organization lose their creativity over time due to the more powerful expectations and behaviors of the surrounding organization. Some of the people in the creative group leave; others sacrifice their creativity in making the compromises necessary to gain acceptance to the larger climate.[5]

Karolczak and Welty built successful, independent, creative groups with distinctly independent climates within larger companies. Fortunately, both executives were prepared to work at maintaining the climates of their groups. Without continual maintenance, climates disappear.

Until it was acquired in December 2001 by SPSS, Inc., the Web analytics software firm NetGenesis had no parent organization to affect its climate. Rather, the company needed to achieve and maintain creativity because it existed in an industry, Internet consulting, that demands constant creativity at the highest level. Cofounder Matt Cutler was adamant that creativity not be left to chance:

> *How does creativity pertain to highly evolving industries? I'm a Darwinist at heart. In a world where strength brings success and you have to have muscles to compete, you learn to lift weights. In markets that require creativity, what muscles do you flex? The most powerful muscles are in the spirit of your company. In world-class companies creativity is ingrained in the climate.*[6]

To survive in the tumultuous world of e-commerce, Cutler and former NetGenesis CEO Larry Bohn "went searching for the brightest, most creative people. A climate of creativity that will be self-perpetuating is born inchoate from the people you hire."[7] The people they chose were among the most skilled, most experienced, and most ambitious in the industry. Of equal importance, the people they chose were also among the most creative in the industry. They expected to work for a company where they could exercise their creativity to the fullest.

In an industry where creativity was a paramount attribute, NetGenesis hired explicitly for creativity. By bringing in a work force already accustomed and inclined to work creatively and to do so successfully, Cutler and Bohn walked creative expectations and behaviors right in the front door.

Then they reinforced the creativity. Bohn says, "Although we don't think you can produce creativity in any organized way, you can find the moments when creativity happens and publicly recognize it, even when it happens by accident."

Cutler designed a "heroes program," called the NetGenesis Rocks Award, that publicly recognized and rewarded risk takers. "In flexing our creative muscles we have to focus on the unique creative abilities of the individual. And we want our organization to be egalitarian. Heroism can come from anyone. It is not the exclusive province of leaders. . . . The things that contribute to long-term creative growth in the individual and in our company get special attention." To stretch staff members beyond their own expertise, for example, the program rewards people who create outside their job descriptions. "We recognize the number cruncher who does promotional or communications work for a charity, which calls for creative growth. If he merely does more numbers crunching for the charity, that's like using the same hammer on a different nail."

Cutler and Bohn had an unusual opportunity, recognized it, and seized it. In an industry that lives or dies by creativity, they were able to find and hire a proven creative work force at the very beginning of their company's life and then build around the work force a climate that supports creativity by institutionalizing the appreciation of it.

Expectations and Behaviors Reinforcing Creativity

In all three situations described, the climate nurtured and supported creativity and the expectation of creative behavior. Employees undertook the creative work, which generated creative expectations in themselves and other employees, who responded by behaving creatively, in turn reinforcing creative expectations. Each climate became a self-reinforcing, virtuous cycle of creative expectations and behaviors. The climates also were a magnet for job seekers with creative talent who wanted a creativity-friendly environment in which to work.

One caution. If you place employees in a position well beyond what they can handle, you set them up for failure. A great researcher may not make a great product developer. Creative failure, just as any other sort, can become its own self-reinforcing cycle of negative expectations and negative behaviors.

Providing Autonomy and Support

Companies that want the behaviors that lead to creativity and innovation must foster the expectations that elicit those behaviors. Autonomy and freedom and support of those who exercise entrepreneurialism in service to a company will, if generously given, advance its climate in the long run.

Autonomy

Many companies organize themselves using a model of a single person in command and a chain of authority that cascades down a hierarchy. Particularly strong command-and-control hierarchies can foster the expectation that independent thought is ignored or even punishable. Employees behave accordingly, avoiding independent thought even when they have the chance to exercise it and discouraging it when they find it in others. This kind of rigid hierarchy in a company discourages creativity in the extreme.

Relaxing the command-and-control model, giving employees broad autonomy rather than narrow command, allows and in fact stimulates creative expectations and creative behavior.[8] In the context of this discussion, autonomy does not mean arbitrary freedom to do anything at all (including nothing at all). For our purposes, autonomy means the freedom to work as you see fit to achieve company goals. Educational psychologist Edward Deci has shown that autonomy in this sense contributes powerfully, far more than does control, to intrinsic motivation, to the learning and self-esteem inherent in curiosity, to creativity in general.[9]

When 3M offers autonomous time for self-initiated projects at work, the company is giving its employees independent responsibility for broad goals and expecting inner-directed effort, creative effort, and productivity in return. When Steelcase invites employees to design a part of their jobs autonomously, it expects a uniquely creative but measurable advance of the company's interest and a stronger creative climate.

Some institutions, rarely businesses, go further than autonomy and offer absolute freedom to high-caliber creators, often despite opposition from outside the institution. The National Institute for the Arts grants monies to artists, even those who defy popular opinion. The tenure system offers total freedom of research, sometimes controversial research, to professors who have proved their ability. Corporations tend to wall off their experiments in total freedom. Hallmark allows its creative artists freedom to study everything from cooking to motorcycle riding during their 30 percent renewal time.[10] Lucent and Microsoft allow free-ranging experiments within their Lucent Labs and Microsoft Labs, respectively.

In a traditional, hierarchical company, midlevel managers who've paid traditional dues on their way up may find autonomy in the ranks harder to accept than do top leaders who want employees to be creative with products and customers. Even a midlevel manager who backs the need for a more creative company may not recognize the degree to which he restricts autonomy. "They can do their job any way they want, so long as it's done right," explained one manager, for whom "done right" meant "in the manner I expect," effectively canceling out the intrinsic motivation at the heart of autonomy. Another manager at the same hierarchical company (a company working to become creative) offered similarly contingent autonomy. "We would exercise authority only if things were going badly." In a competitive world where things can go badly on a weekly basis, employees working under this manager will not be able to exercise their autonomy for long enough for it to have a creative impact.

The solution lies first in recognizing the potential of the command-and-control hierarchy to foster a climate in which the cycle of expectations and behavior discourages creativity. Then comes commitment to relaxing the command and control in favor of more employee autonomy. Such a commitment demands resolve, patience, getting the message out, and cheerleading. We will discuss this at length in chapter 6.

Organizational Support

Employees given autonomy have the space to gain intrinsic motivation and the creative curiosity that follows. The exercise of autonomy, the creative behavior that fulfills creative expectations, needs organizational support.

In the creative effort at any company, people play at the edge of their familiar universe—sometimes momentarily, sometimes for months—putting together something that, for them, has never been conceived before. Then they take the new creation back for evaluation to the organization, where an established web of expectations probably resists the newness of the concept.

Some people have the innate confidence to offer big ideas aimed at large-scale change. Others, regardless of the size of their inspiration, naturally take a chance only on smaller, less risky ideas that they know will encounter less resistance. And many people, no matter how creative, take no chance at all. The worth of new ideas, however, has little correlation to the courage of their creator. Timid people imagine just as remarkably and, with encouragement, create just as profoundly as assertive people. If a company is to tap the full creative wealth of all its talent, some measure of conscious organizational support is needed for all its employees.

When Grafix, a computer monitor manufacturer, understood that it needed to build an entirely new business, it put its brightest, strongest, most flexible, most imaginative people to work starting up the new business. But none of them had started a company before, and they would never have done so without support. Grafix recognized that these people were not entrepreneurs. They did not possess the vision, drive, and confidence to leap without hesitation into newer, riskier jobs, into an entirely new company. They needed resources—money, space, access to information, and a base to work from. And they needed the expertise of people familiar with start-ups.

But these sorts of resources alone were not enough support for people who were otherwise satisfied with the jobs they already had, along with the security and status these jobs gave them. The final piece of support they needed was the parent company's guarantee that they could have their old jobs back if the new venture failed. With this assurance, fear and tentativeness subsided, and creative curiosity could be engaged. Knowing that there was a safety net, the group could set up the new company as creatively as possible and be sure that when they took the shape of the new company back to the parent company for evaluation, they wouldn't be out of a job if the new company didn't survive. The parent company had provided autonomy with the corresponding expectation of creativity. It had also provided the support to make creative behavior possible. Both autonomy and support are necessary to complete the creative climate.

Producer Peter McGhee, the vice president for national programming at WGBH, the public television station in Boston, maintains a climate that supports creativity to a high degree. He encourages artists and producers to create bold programs, and he encourages them get up and go on after a failure. He also actively champions their work to sponsors. When a company and its leaders join employees to push the employees' ideas out into the world, employees get more than autonomy and support; they get a measure of affirmation that creates yet an additional degree of motivation. In this climate, expectations and behavior answer back and forth in a continuing escalation of creative well-being. Programs guided by Peter McGhee have earned WGBH more than fifty Emmy Awards, thirty-seven Peabody Awards for broadcast excellence, and twenty-five duPont-Columbia journalism awards.

Large-Scale Climate Change

Creative climates are easiest to construct at an organization's inception, as Pete Karolczak at Hewlett-Packard and the founders of NetGenesis did, or on a small scale, as David Welty did. Changing the climate of an entire established company is harder. But when a company fully commits to new behavior and new expectations, the old self-reinforcing behaviors and expectations will in time begin to weaken and break up, allowing the new patterns to take hold. If the company's commitment holds firm through the disorienting period of fragmentation, the change will accelerate until the new set of behaviors and expectations are in place and that new climate in turn becomes self-reinforcing. Again, such commitment is not easy.

More than forty years ago, in *The Human Side of Enterprise,* Douglas MacGregor challenged the command-and-control assumptions of the business establishment: "The distinctive potential contribution of the human being . . . at every level of the organization stems from his capacity to think, to plan, to exercise judgment, to be creative, to direct and control his own behavior."[11]

MacGregor was arguing on behalf of the creative climate. Today, while there has been much progress, too few leaders ask and expect creativity of their employees; too few leaders provide the climate in which creativity can flourish.

FIVE

Personal Creative Climate: The Bubble

THE IDEAL CREATIVE CLIMATE nurtures intrinsic motivation, assures the safety necessary for curiosity, holds high expectations for creativity, and provides the support critical to evaluation. But even in an ideal climate, the ability of individual employees to achieve full creative potential depends on their ability to create their own internal climate and to influence the immediate climate around them.

A company climate ideal for creativity is not commonplace. Many fine companies consider themselves creative but lack climates that adequately enhance the creative individual. And regardless of company efforts, the pressures of competitive business can generate levels of anxiety that might defeat anyone's creativity. It is the protection and enhancement of a personal creative climate that allows individuals to accomplish their creative work within large company climates—both those that are sympathetic to the creative individual and those that are not.

Carol Previte, an account director at Jack Morton World-wide, described a typical situation in communication firms:

Last week one of our designers was on a production deadline. With just twenty-four hours to go, he still had no copy to work with. He knew he was going to get only one shot at designing something the client would love. As we were coming down to the wire, he turned to me with a grin and said, "This would make a great war story." This guy's sense of humor has always kept him going.[1]

The designer's humor in fact supported his personal creative climate. The ability to be amused in tough times is often innate, but it is worth consciously developing. The designer used this ability to provide himself with the emotional safety he needed to produce creatively under intense pressure.

Creative anxieties are hardly unique to the communications industry. When Bankers Trust—a creatively oriented bank—was merged with the larger, more traditional Deutsche Bank, Darcy Bradbury worried about being able to remain creative: "Bankers Trust was older and smaller, while the new bank is much more bureaucratic and political. We don't know the rules in the new culture yet, or how to get around them." Bradbury's job was to pursue acquisitions for the bank. "In the old bank I had the space to form deals and make concessions as needed. There are more obstacles to that kind of freewheeling autonomy in the new system. To pursue the acquisitions I think are right, I am going to have to work hard to reestablish my freedom in the larger bank and to justify the risks I need to take. That's going to take some time."[2]

Adding to the difficulty of shifting into a more conservative culture was the fact that the merger, like many, led to layoffs. Fear and anxiety levels rose among Bradbury's staff, compounding the diminished risk taking and new initiatives, at least at first. Bradbury had confidence in her own creative ability, however, confidence that was part of the personal creative climate she brought with her from the old Banker's Trust. Because of this confidence, she was able to envision reaching out from her own secure creative bubble to ameliorate the larger climate immediately surrounding her department. "The new bank is a good one and ultimately fair, and I think staff anxiety is subsiding. Once I create some stability in my department and pockets of stability start to emerge in the surrounding areas, we'll be able to move forward again, building a department as flexible and creative as the old one."

Even entrepreneurial organizations that pride themselves on their creative, nonhierarchical organization can stifle creativity. According to Marylyn Dintenfass, creative director at a Web site development company, "Our president wants this company to represent the cutting edge of innovation in our marketplace. He knows we need to be creative in order to attract the major talents of our generation."[3] As a result, the company approaches projects from multiple perspectives and encourages department heads from its three divisions, strategy, creative, and technical, to consult and reach consensus on every client problem.

The intent is to encourage creativity on all sides of a project and then to honor the creativity in a consensual solution. But as Dintenfass explains, the compromises demanded by consensus constrain individual creative input. "Sometimes the intuitive, holistic visionary view of the original creator gets lost, pushed aside by the process of consensus. A parallel reality has emerged here. Project heads may think that the process is working perfectly while the artists may feel marginalized. There really is nothing to protect the creativity of the individual, artist or otherwise." In a climate of consensus, the individual needs a particularly strong personal creative climate to sustain his or her personal intrinsic motivation and singular risk-taking curiosity.

The Bubble

Dintenfass, Bradbury, and Previte work, like most people, in situations where they must fight to keep personal creativity alive for their own good and for the good of their companies. They have learned through experience that they and their staff can and often must sustain their creative abilities by wrapping a personal creative climate—a personal bubble made of protective sympathies, analogous to the ideal creative corporate climate—around the constellation of their own subjective creative virtues. Like an invisible shield, the bubble of a personal creative climate insulates people from the indifference or hostility of the larger climate.

While your protective bubble, or personal protective climate, enhances your creative ability, the bubble to a large extent depends on your mastery of the creative dynamics. The clearer and stronger your motivation, the stronger your bubble. The more your curiosity is aroused and engaged, the stronger the bubble. The more effective your connection breaking and making, the stronger the bubble. And the stronger the bubble, the better able you are to accept a negative assessment of your ideas as an impetus for further problem solving rather than as a reason to abandon the creative process.

In the same way that larger climates operate through expectation and behavior, individuals know what they can expect from themselves and what behaviors of their own will help them meet those expectations. Once you have begun to make a conscious effort at creativity and have developed a sense of a personal creative worth, your sophistication in personal creativity can begin to grow. You will know the history and nature of your motivation and your curiosity; you will know how and why you approach the breaking and making of connections and what evaluation can mean on a personal level.

As we said in chapter 2, the more people have a sense of their creative profile, the more able they are to bring the creative process fully into play. Going a step further, the more deeply an individual understands his or her personal creative profile, the more he or she will be able to create circumstances in which the profile will flourish. The wealth of intimate, subjective self-knowledge and the determination to use it for one's own protection can counteract creativity-sapping forces in a larger work climate, giving an individual a critical measure of control over his or her own creativity.

Just as athletes work to master not only their physical skills but also the frame of mind that allows them to perform to their ability, so creatively healthy people must maintain and continually improve the frame of mind that allows them to perform as best they can creatively. To this end, they shape a personal creative climate or bubble. As creative successes outnumber failures, self-confidence and personal satisfaction grow into expectation that elicits more successful behavior. This satisfaction cycles back to further nourish expectation and reinforce the bubble of the personal creative climate.

How do you translate an understanding of your personal creative profile into the protective bubble that promotes a creative climate? Look again at the clues to what motivates, intrigues, frightens, or intimidates you. Some people need independence to develop intrinsic motivation toward project goals; some people get their most creative ideas in interchange with others. If you are someone whose creative profile shows a need for independence, the trick is to personally assume the responsibility for evoking independence within yourself. Don't wait for the larger, exterior company climate to provide it. If you're someone who needs interchange with others—whether competitive or collaborative—arrange to spend time with others who inspire your creativity when you're faced with high-pressure demands for a solution.

Conrad Paulus at AT&T research knows that his best work comes from argument. So he searches out peers, some in other companies, with whom he can have a rigorous back-and-forth. Rick Hensler, a former creative director at Universal Studios, needs the collaborative stimulation of others for his creative thinking. "It's when ideas are popping around me that my own ideas come to me," he says, so he often invites others to work with him.[4] If laughter helps you to break and make connections under pressure, as it does a designer at Jack Morton, generate that laughter for yourself.

People who want to improve and control their ability to exercise creativity need to work to strengthen their own creative climate at deep levels. When Will Novosedlik was at Russell Branding, he struggled against a deeply ingrained defensiveness, knowing that the defensiveness undermined his ability to deliver his best creative product. "When you collaborate with others, your own self-defenses can kill your creativity. I'm a defensive person and have a tendency to see criticism as an attack. It takes faith, trust, and risk to lay yourself open, invite the response of another person or team, and really listen to it."[5] Annie Gaudreault, also at Russell Branding, forced herself into the creative milieu when she felt that she was herself profoundly uncreative. As a result, she developed a degree of creative confidence that served as her personal creative climate bubble, a bubble that was strengthened as she let her colleagues catch her when she slid back into judgmental habits.

Expecting Success

Expectations are fundamental to the personal creative climate. A person who expects that the problem at hand is solvable, and that he or she is capable of crafting the solution, will find that expectation shapes his awareness and performance in productive ways. When you expect that what you are working on will have a successful outcome, you more readily dip into resources and energy you would not otherwise expend because you believe the extra effort will be rewarded. Expectations become self-fulfilling. With each new success, confidence and competence and expectations grow, which in turn leads to more ambitious challenges.[6]

Athletes know that envisioning themselves playing better, rehearsing each move mentally, reinforces their expectations and boosts their performance.[7] So too in creative efforts: People who envision and expect creative results in their work get creative results more often than people who do not.

Psychologist Mihaly Csikszentmihalyi reports that when managers, peers, or the community expect high creative output from someone, they get it more often than when they don't expect it.[8] Similarly, when individuals have high expectations for their own creativity, they tend to fulfill the expectations.

Self-fulfilling expectations are important at several stages of creativity—when ideas are created and when they're implemented. Rick Hensler, while he was at Universal Studios, considered himself "an idea man." When the Islands of Adventure theme park was being planned, he cranked out hundreds of ideas for rides and attractions, and he did it confidently because he had done it successfully so many times before. When it came time to implement the ideas, Mark Woodbury, Islands of Adventure's creative director, led his team in developing countless concepts, the best of which they fearlessly drew on for implementation. Although much of their work was untried and cost millions of dollars, the team was comfortable with its ability to create on demand, despite working on a very intimidating scale.[9] As a result of their creative work and that of others at Universal Studios, attendance at Universal parks gained 17 percent on the Walt Disney Company's Florida parks between 2000 and 2002.[10] Both men have succeeded time after time, taking on ever more challenging tasks during their careers. They were fed, while they were creating and implementing, by the ascending and continuing life of their self-fulfilling expectations.

Unfortunately, personal expectations can fail to materialize, and failure can be problematic. After Peter McGhee's producer got worse reviews than she expected, she could not recover positive expectations for her work; she was unable to launch another project. Salesmen who miss a target can get into a slump and lose the confidence that's so important in selling.

Individuals who don't want to sabotage their own creative climate bubble should try to keep expectations high but within reason. Universal's Hensler and Woodbury could not keep their creative expectations for long if they expected colossal success in microbiology or even if they had expected to take on a major amusement park when they were just out of college. The television producer might have been able to produce again if she had not expected too much of reviews too early in her career or if she had put her expectations on the relative quality of her work rather than its reception by reviewers.

As with success, failure breeds expectation of more failure, which can also become self-fulfilling.[11] When you fail, you have to reassess expectations and try to build into your bubble your own system of encouragement. Salesmen who need to be creative in how they attract clients or close sales get out of a slump more quickly if they focus on their proven strengths and their past successes. If they're able to set realistic sales goals, they can begin once more to reinforce expectations of success.

The Power of Passion

Passion strengthens a personal creative climate. Nancy Leaming, president of Tufts Health Care Plan, reflected seriously on her personal values before starting work with THCP and realized that she had a passion for treating people right. So she felt a calling to go aboard at THCP, where treating people right meant not just courtesy and convenience, important as those are, but also getting patients healthy and keeping them healthy. Leaming communicated her customer service ethos from the day she joined the company—at meetings, in memos, and in conversations with employees.[12]

According to Maureen Arkle, a vice president at THCP, "Not everyone in the organization had that particular enthusiasm, of course, but those who did became excited enough to rouse others to join in. As others became engaged and excited, their motivation increased and their personal creativity was activated." Tufts Health Care Plan, the second biggest health plan in New England, attributes its success to this passion. "Many things are alike in our business," says Arkle, "but the kind of quality customer service we created is what distinguished us."

Leaming did not decide to acquire her passion to treat people right; it was there inside her, something that she had as a child and that she recognized and valued as an adult. She cultivated the motivating passion for treating people right as a component in her personal creative climate bubble. She deployed it as the crucial characteristic of the larger, companywide atmosphere she fostered at THCP. Leaming's passion worked for her, and it worked for her company.

As well as being able to impart their values beyond themselves, people driven by passion can develop a local climate that supports higher energy for more imaginative and more productive breaking and making of connections. Bob Miller, president of

Correctnet, a Web design company, always liked to do things fast and get the most out of what he did; he had a passion for speed and for leverage. This passion guided and supported his business pursuits and practices. Early on, when planning to create Web sites for individual doctors' offices, he conceived an interactive medical query system that would allow patients to get fast access to information about common ailments and remedies. Miller then designed a generic Web site around this interactive query system. He sold it to doctors, customizing it to fit each office and leveraging the cost through the broad participation of other doctors. As a result, thousands of doctors' offices could handle routine patient queries faster and more easily than previously imaginable. Miller used the virtues of the Internet to leverage an idea for a time-based product into widespread application.

Miller has also leveraged his staffing as Correctnet has developed variations on this formula in industry after industry. Of the 115 people in the company, seventy-five perform client services. Each of the seventy-five has come from another career and a lower pay scale than that of most e-commerce marketing professionals. As Miller explains, "We hire schoolteachers, ex-bank employees, and homemakers who are trying to jump into today's electronic business. Without the help we give them, they couldn't make the switch."[13] With 20 percent of each service employee's time allocated to training, Miller has eight full-time trainers on the staff to teach the seventy-five people tools, design, strategy, sales, and small business issues. "When people leave Correctnet," Miller claims, "they can get jobs anywhere else in the Web industry."

Miller takes smart, willing, underutilized, inexpensive talent and applies his money, training, and attention in such a way that seventy-five people perform happily and productively at a level equivalent to that of people paid three times the salary Miller pays. Miller leverages money, effort, and native intelligence to get good, inexpensive production. The employees leverage their intelligence and their willingness to learn to leap onto a higher platform than they could otherwise reach. And because these retooled employees are involved in Web design as well as customer interactions,

Miller can leverage his more expensive technical staff: "Ten technical people are all we need to serve 1,500 clients."

Miller also applies his passion for speed to managing the employees' time. There is a rule at Correctnet that work on any problem that takes more than three days to solve must be scrapped. "I mean delete it completely, wipe it, hit shift-delete," emphasizes Miller. "If it takes that long, the problem is too big, too complex, or we didn't atomize it correctly. I want them to learn the lessons of speed." Miller purposely wastes the work to elicit the "instinct for discarding and rapid redevelopment." Two outcomes that are always applauded and never punished are "fast failure and radical approaches."

Miller has seen his employees' courage, skills, and speed grow. He's also seen his passion for speed and leverage contribute to a personal climate that energizes him to drive a successful new model of business in a highly competitive environment.

Besides inspiring, passion sustains, as Elizabeth Deane discovered when producing her documentary on Nixon. "It wasn't just another idea. I knew I *had* to do a film on this man."[14] Her passion reinforced the bubble of her personal creative climate as she fought to overcome the obstacles to a most unlikely creative project.

Reaching Outside the Bubble

Even people with the strongest personal creative climates need support from outside themselves to accomplish goals. The relationship between the personal creative climate and the surrounding climate is complementary: If both are barren, little creativity results; if one is supportive and the other not, creative results are likely to be uneven; if both are richly supportive, creative thinking blooms.

If you want to increase personal creative performance, you need to consider the task from the two perspectives. You need to know what you can bring to the table and what the larger climate has to bring. You need to know which internal factors you can provide to nurture and protect your creative profile. And you need to know which external factors critically amplify or dampen your creative ability. Then you have to determine which of the external factors you can change and which you will have to tolerate.

The external climate you need for peak creativity is unique to you. As an extension of understanding your personal creative profile, build a baseline of knowledge about the most sympathetic external climate by noting the external climate during the times you feel stimulated or otherwise. Some of Dave Welty's artists, for example, flourished in a fast, competitive environment while others wilted. In her television production offices, Elizabeth Deane always dressed in a style that "could pass for business clothes, in case I had to meet a funder on short notice," while business management author Tom Peters "couldn't write a creative word in a suit if it was my last day on earth."[15] J. K. Rowling reportedly wrote her Harry Potter books in coffee shops because she wanted warmth and could write in the midst of people and activity; others need peace and quiet.[16]

We recommend that people whose livelihood depends on creativity, their own and that of those around them, examine what influences personal creative climates so that they can customize the local climates. Marylyn Dintenfass, at her Web site development company, found that a climate of forced dialogue and consensus destroyed the singular vision of some creative people in her organization. Carol Previte, at Jack Morton Worldwide, discovered that some artists who work well in teams cannot work in the presence of a strong individual artist. After Dintenfass and Previte observed their workplace closely, they adjusted for creativity.

Corporate Climates
Adapting to Personal Climates

Leaders cannot adjust the creative climate of a company specifically for each individual, but they can develop an overall climate friendly to the creativity of the largest number of employees. If that climate has enough flexibility, then employees can make the smaller adjustments necessary to suit their own bubble of personal creative climate.

Climates that serve employees' creativity poorly are characterized by strict adherence to procedure, overemphasis on precedent and analysis, response to office politics instead of personal merits, automatic reliance on past solutions, and excessive imitation of the strategies of other companies. A healthy climate for creativity shows itself with the frequent appearance of new, undeveloped ideas, easy humor, focus on ideas rather than careers, comfort with ambiguity, and enthusiasm for new opportunities.

Leaders modeling behavior that supports creativity can make a real difference in promoting creatively useful expectations. Leaders who spend time listening to and building on new ideas demonstrate in the most important way their organization's friendliness toward risk and creativity. Leaders who shake up their own physical surroundings in the interest of creativity, as did executives at Steelcase when they opened up their offices, give the same powerful message.

Companies that don't actively support creativity need to realize that individuals who receive little reward and support for creative work will reduce their creative efforts.[17] And the best creative employees, if frustrated in their ability to reach peak creativity, will leave for another climate.

The good news is that we have found individuals at every level in every company who can and often do take personal responsibility for shaping their own productive bubble of personal creative climate. Exercising this responsibility serves the individual employee well. And the presence of strong creative bubbles compounds the return on investment for organizations that provide a companywide creative climate.

Part Three

Action

SIX

Leadership: Fostering Systemic Creativity

GUIDANT, INC., a Silicon Valley and Midwest manufac-turer of medical equipment including defibrillators, stents, and pacemakers, was formed from the merger of several entre-preneurial businesses. Its leaders wanted to maintain its entrepre-neurial character. The company had grown large enough that bureaucracy threatened to dampen the speed, risk taking, and collegial atmosphere of the original start-ups. Kathy Lundberg, a vice president, described the company's predicament:

We could see some of the entrepreneurial nature of our company fading, and we knew we needed to catch it in time. We were lucky to have a base of entrepreneurial experience still alive in the company; many of the people who started or had been part of the original companies were still here in-house. But we knew

*we could lose those people and that entrepreneurial nature as we
scaled up. And we knew that if we lost those people and that culture, if we didn't stay creative and innovative, then the company
itself would not survive.*[1]

Unlike Steelcase, which was inspired by market demands into
multiple experiments as it found its way to meaningful change,
Guidant felt that they could take a less pressured and more holistic approach. The firm's leaders decided first to assess the current
state of creativity in the organization. So among other efforts, they
convened employee focus groups around the company, asking
employees to identify what they saw as barriers to entrepreneurial
behavior. As Lundberg later recounted, "We heard things like
there were too many people involved in every decision, that failure
was so risky people didn't want to try anything new, and that
company leaders didn't listen and did what they wanted anyway."

Guidant also looked to companies with reputations for ongoing creativity. Representatives researched Sony, Motorola, 3M,
and Disney, among others, to see which creativity strategies those
organizations employed. They took stock of their own company's
creative profile and compared it to the company's needs and what
they observed in other companies. Guidant leaders also went outside the company and brought in a consultant for help with the
tricky questions involved in large-scale change.

The leaders then examined different models of corporate
structure that raise the levels of creative behavior, and finally they
made a plan for their own company. "Ultimately," Lundberg explained, "we decided on a three-pronged approach—top-down,
bottom-up, and 'brushfire teams'—all working simultaneously
over a two- to three-year period."

The top-down approach involved a series of seminars on
entrepreneurship, supportive management, and problem solving.
At first the seminars were given to the 280 most senior leaders.
Within the first year the training cascaded down to the next 450
managers. Beverly Mehlhoff, a director, explained the focus of the
effort: "Our idea of management had to change from one of com-

mand and control, which closes down creative thought in the ranks, to one of coaching, which opens it up. Our leaders learned as a body to listen to and appreciate the ideas of the people in this company."[2]

The bottom-up approach was orchestrated by Emerson Martlage, a vice president. It included everyone in several functions in one business group. The first training effort was focused on personal transformation and run by an external training organization. "The idea," explained Martlage, "is for everyone to learn to understand that they are responsible people in a changing world, to show them how they can take control of their lives and their work, and how to speak what they believe."[3] The next round of training is planned to focus directly on building skills for creativity and innovation, skills that can be applied for personal growth and the company's benefit by both individuals and groups.

The top-down and bottom-up approaches worked simultaneously to complement each other. As employees learned the skills to think creatively, leaders learned to encourage creative thought and the sharing of ideas.

The third segment of Guidant's approach established "brushfire teams," a name for teams that undertook products or processes that generated immediate value—but that also served as hands-on laboratories for learning about creativity. The teams identified and monitored factors that appeared to lead to entrepreneurial success and then reported on the factors to the company. One team, for example, was given charge of making a higher-density capacitor, the largest physical component in the company's defibrillators. Luke Cristensen, an engineer and member of the team, elaborated on the process:

> We each have more work to do than just this high-density mini-capacitor, but we're allowed the freedom to zig and zag daily as we need in order to adapt to this brushfire project. Now, fifteen months into it, we're ahead of the competition in minicapacitors and expect to widen the lead. We all think differently, and I don't think that we have ever come to consensus about

anything, but we developed a style of working together that worked for us and will continue to enhance other projects.[4]

To reward the team and to encourage others, the team was recognized in promotional videos of the company's creative work.

In 1999 Guidant broke into *Fortune*'s list of the 100 best companies to work for, at number 31. Now the company that Kathy Lundberg worried would lose its best thinkers and most entrepreneurial individuals is instead holding on to those thinkers and entrepreneurs and growing more of them internally, while attracting still more from across the industry.

Systemic creativity is a never-ending quest. Guidant continues to struggle at times to maintain momentum in the quest. No company, certainly not Guidant, claims complete and final creative success. Nonetheless, Guidant's leaders envision systemic creativity, and the company is on the way to achieving it.

Leaders of other companies also aim for systemic creativity. In the following pages of this chapter, we describe a few strong actions that almost any company leader can take to effect a company's change toward creativity. As we explore these disciplines, we revisit familiar creative concepts, but with a focus on effecting change. This requires different and deeper understanding of the material we covered earlier. Although we initially presented the creative dynamics in sequence, the creative process is best understood as a whole. And it is best learned experientially, like riding a bike, rather than academically. Every chance to learn the process from a different angle makes for more complete comprehension. To learn from the perspective of a leader committing a company into systemic creativity is to get a practical feel for creativity.

At the time when the industrial age came into full flower, the management approach—described forty years ago by theorist Douglas McGregor as Theory X—was that employees needed to be controlled to produce good work.[5] Company policies and structures were designed around the assumption that employees responded to extrinsic motivation or even coercion and were not be trusted to be self-directed.

In contrast, corporate leaders emerging from today's business schools have been encouraged to value McGregor's Theory Y management approach—employees want and need to excel and in the right organizational climate will do so. But despite Theory Y, hierarchical, paternalistic attitudes still permeate many businesses of every size today. Management's approach continues to be that position equals knowledge and intelligence and power, that the higher the position the better the ideas, that only someone with formal authority can responsibly handle decisions.

The effect of this management approach is to reduce the creative power of a 30,000-person organization to the top 100 leaders, a power reduction of 300 to 1. To install systemic creativity, leaders must engage the other 29,900 employees. In sum, leaders need to confer the responsibility and capability of creative leadership on every employee. When each employee can engage with the creative process, when each employee feels the need and the chance to perform as a creative leader in the course of his or her work, the company as a whole has begun to reach systemic creativity. It can then concentrate on fine-tuning the system, raising the level of creative ability, and turning creativity into successful innovation.

To foster creativity companywide, companies must: Reduce unnecessary controls; adopt creativity-friendly reward systems; instill new attitudes about efficiency and failure; communicate the value of creative change; provide both the tangible and the intangible resources necessary to creativity; and lead with a guide's attentiveness rather than a manager's command and control.

Reduced Controls

Corporate controls are given and received as either commands (which, in motivation terms, will at best function as extrinsic motivators) or as guidelines (which promote intrinsic motivation). Command control, in Theory X management, not only supercedes any individual's inclination to leadership, it also blocks individuals and their ideas from reaching one another and stimulating creativity among the greatest possible number of people. Possibilities with great promise may never emerge because the people who could realize the promise can't get from one room to another to share the necessary information.

When a company offers flexible guidelines, leaving the interpretation of the guidelines to employees, it honors and stimulates employee intelligence, judgment, and creativity. Jerry McAllister, technical director at 3M, describes a flexible, universal guideline at 3M: "Each person in each business unit is expected to think and act in terms of *foresight,* our term for the continual search for emerging customer needs."[6] The goal of this guideline is clear, and 3M provides and supports latitude for implementation. Employees at 3M know that they have a good chance of receiving the necessary resources if they can explain how their idea will enhance a growth area and meet underserved customer needs.

3M also issues commands. One is that mainly scientists and technical people—and only limited marketing people—may attend internal technology fairs. This command is intended to allow the free exploration of technologies among a broad spectrum of 3M experts, while guarding against the possibility of people with limited knowledge of patent laws jeopardizing the proprietary strengths of 3M.[7]

Boundaries between functions—reinforced by corporate structures and procedures—often prevent the flow of information needed for the most encompassing creative thought and innovation. When segregation occurs vertically in a company, it produces functional or product or divisional silos. When it occurs horizontally, it leads to layering, isolating similar people in strata based on professions or other hierarchical levels.

Once boundaries form, groups within the silo or the stratum tend to institute procedures that reinforce the segregation. Scientists share information among themselves, stimulating each other to greater heights of pure experiment, but then they must toss their inventions over the functional wall to marketing. The marketing people figure out how best to get the new product to market.

The goal of functional specialization is for the association of peers to produce a collective excellence. In fact, not only does the potential for creative synergy between groups get lost, but boundaries and separation often foster mutual distrust and poor working relationships.

3M offsets the effects of isolating technological information in the prepatent stage by giving the information broad disclosure once legal usage protection is assured. Their global information system credo is "Technologies belong to the whole company." As soon as any aspect of technology receives release for disclosure, any of 3M's laboratories worldwide can use it and in turn contribute their own experiments to the communication system, speeding global learning. Marketing and sales have full access to the information system and add their own perspective to it for the benefit of all their colleagues.

For 3M, the isolation of information and the concurrent separation of technology and marketing is temporary. In the many companies where isolation and separation are more than temporary and not absolutely necessary, leaders need, as much as feasible, to do away with it. Leaders can minimize the effect of isolation through a wide range of actions, including widening the list of people invited to certain forums, instituting rotational assignments, rewarding cross-boundary collaboration, and commissioning problem solving that requires boundaries to be crossed (for instance, how can brands in the candy category be used in other categories?). In the next chapter, we'll see how Nabisco crossed just such category boundaries.

Tufts Health Care Plan addresses boundary issues in part by eliminating them; for example, it operates without a new products department, so every department has a responsibility to generate new product ideas for itself and for the company as a whole. The aim is to stimulate creativity throughout the company. As Steve Leichtman explains, "If we labeled one department as creative, we would be telling the other departments that creativity isn't their business—and we believe it's the business of every person in the company.[8] THCP operates without a strategy department for similar reasons. Jon Kingsdale, executive in charge of strategy, says that his role is to ensure widespread awareness of important information and to coordinate a strategic process that involves all managers.[9]

At 3M, according to William Coyne, senior vice president for research and development, now retired, "The first principle is the promotion of entrepreneurship and insistence on freedom in the workplace to pursue innovative ideas." This is also the principle behind 3M's allotting 15 percent of employees' time to projects of their own invention, projects that routinely spark collaborative coalitions involving individuals from a range of different departments and strata in the hierarchy.

As the controls and procedures that separate employees from information and from one another disappear, employees gain higher potential to create as they have access to more diverse information.

Creativity-Friendly Rewards

Leaders can foster creativity throughout the company by using an effective reward policy as a supplement to normal wages and salaries. Rewards are often used to steer employee behavior, but studies find that promises of money or promotion tend to increase focus on the intended goal at the expense of creativity. Employees who pursue extrinsic rewards simultaneously forgo exploration. They simply take the fastest path to the desired end. The sooner they reach the goal, the sooner they get the reward, and the sooner they start to go for the next reward.[10] Promises of extrinsic rewards discourage sharing information, collaboration that could augment creativity and lead to better solutions. "If we gave monetary rewards, people would close their notebooks to protect their ideas," says 3M's Geoff Nicholson.[11]

Recognition as a reward, on the other hand, encourages the curiosity-seeking, risk-taking, and connection-making behaviors coincident with creative thinking.[12] When financial rewards are used as recognition rather than bait, they too encourage future creative behavior. 3M, for instance, offers monetary awards as recognition, but no one can expect a monetary award while doing the work.

Sometimes, creativity-friendly rewards actually fund future creative work. For instance, the MacArthur grants, awarded annually, are unrestricted fellowships that honor individuals who have shown "extraordinary originality and dedication in their creative pursuits, and a marked capacity for self-direction" in social, scientific, or artistic endeavors. The grants are peer-nominated and are unencumbered—that is, no future work is required over the five-year award period.[13] In most cases recipients continue doing what they were doing, as they were not working for the MacArthur grant to begin with. The funding gives them more resources to follow their passion more fully. These financial rewards do not say, "If you do this, I'll give you that." The rewards recognize and encourage employees at all levels not to bypass creativity to reach goals but to engage creativity in reaching them.

New Attitudes About Efficiency and Failure

Business tends to like efficiency and loathe failure. Leaders who instill systemic creativity in companies do not have to abandon those values, but we advise them to develop an appreciation of the fact that while creativity brings long-term benefits, some inefficiency accompanies creativity. In the same vein, leaders need to institutionalize a sympathetic understanding that failure in small doses is less expensive than the cost of losing out to other companies' creativity.

Efficiency

The industrial revolution raised efficiency to a science. Once maximum efficiency was established, most procedures became standard, and attention turned to other business tasks. Procedure other than the standard was perceived as a threat to efficiency and thus to the profits and productivity derived from efficiency.

But the benefits of creativity—new initiatives, new designs, new programs, new products—do not arrive in an efficient manner. They rarely work smoothly at first and cannot be standardized at the outset. Leaders need to make it clear to the company that short-term inefficiencies of the creative process are quite likely and need to be managed sensitively. For example, to maintain unambiguous commitment to meeting short-term operating profit goals, one might decide to fund creativity on a separate level.

Even the most creative companies have to guard against emphasizing efficiency at the expense of creativity. One vice president at a medical equipment corporation still sees executives tinkering with the systems they oversee until they've managed the inefficiencies, including the creative inefficiencies, right out of them. He argues for a balance that will allow his company to maintain its creative effort. He values efficiency, but says, "we have to know when to stop."

Failure

3M's oft-quoted former chairman, William L. McKnight, said, "Those men and women to whom we delegate authority and responsibility are going to want to do their jobs in their own way. Mistakes will be made, but if a person is essentially right, the mistakes he or she makes are not as serious in the long run as the mistakes management will make if it is dictatorial and undertakes to tell those under its authority exactly how they must do their job."[14]

This sort of broad tolerance for failures powerfully reinforces individual thinking and initiative in personal creativity. It is the sort of reinforcement needed to successfully instill systemic creativity in any company. But the process is not easy, since many employees are accustomed to controls and strong hierarchy. They will not necessarily believe that the company wants them to step forward and take significant creative initiative.

Eventually, though, if leaders persist in encouraging individual initiative and in expressing tolerance for failure, people will act on their own initiative and sometimes fail. The company's response to the initiative and failure will shape the scope of initiative assumed by other employees in the future.

In the creative process itself, ideas and experiments can generate a seemingly confusing array of possibilities that detract from familiar productivity goals. And many of the possibilities will necessarily fail. The first senior executive who reaches the limit of his tolerance for such confusion and failure may call a halt to creative effort and to the personal initiative that produced it. One way to prevent this short-circuiting is to spread responsibility among several executives at key stages of evaluation and judgment so that no one executive faces the messiness of creativity alone, especially at a point where he can derail wholesale the changes that embody systemic creativity. Another answer, as used by Guidant, is to provide training in the creative process to management. And Hallmark established an office of innovation that was staffed with professionals adept at helping "stuck" managers.

3M asserts that many new product ventures never leave the first stages of incubation. William Coyne goes further: "We have failures from every function, every department. And we've had some colossal ones. Back in the 'twenties, one of our top inventors had this incredible flash of brilliance: Maybe people could use sandpaper as a replacement for razor blades. Not surprisingly, this idea never panned out, but the inventor was never punished for pursuing the idea." This unruffled openness about failure frees staff to take risks in the open, admit when the experiment didn't work, learn from it, and apply the learning to new endeavors.[15]

When Harvard Business School professor Rosabeth Moss Kanter conducted her "apples to lemons" research, comparing project successes and failures across companies, she expected that the study would reveal new information on good practices. She was surprised that she found few examples of failures, in spite of research indicating that fewer than 5 percent of new product launches are successful. "Why so few?" she wondered. She then hypothesized that the fear of admitting failure, the repositioning of failures as successes, the absence of risk taking, the aborting of projects early on, and cover-ups accounted for most of the missing failures.[16]

Business leaders have a hard time accepting, much less encouraging, failures. Yet people who perform at or beyond the edge of familiar knowledge, people who take creative risks, have to fail a significant portion of the time. Employees who have tried, failed, and come back to try again are valuable assets. Most of them enjoy the challenge and willingly step up to the plate again on new projects, with more wisdom and a better handle on their own creative dynamics. These people become educated innovators, tempered risk takers, leaders and managers of creativity of the best sort.

A recent business magazine article reported, "Net entrepreneurs whose companies have tanked, those whose companies have survived, and the VCs who have backed both kinds all say they wouldn't hold failure against a founder whose company goes under. In fact, they say they'd probably consider the person more qualified when it comes to knowing what—and what not—to do."[17] Company leaders who take and maintain a public stance of tolerance for failure display a courage that's fundamental to systemic creativity in any company.

Communicating the Value of Creative Change

Controls, extrinsic rewards, efficiency, and aversion to failure are so ingrained in the usual company that deemphasizing them takes time. Leaders who want to speed up the change to systemic creativity need to aggressively communicate the understanding that a new attitude exists. Employees need to receive and believe the message that creativity is a company priority for creative behavior to follow.

To make it happen, publicly encourage creative performers, both in person and institutionally. Set up an agency to broadcast throughout the company news on the practice and theory and accomplishments of the company's creativity as regularly and enthusiastically as a town crier. Broadcast and promote challenges to creative effort that will inspire ambitious employees.

Encouraging Performers

In systemically creative companies, individuals and teams perform creative work daily. As part of their employees' audience, company leaders should regularly demonstrate appreciation for creative performance.

The most meaningful appreciation can be given one on one. Roger Appledorn, a recently retired scientist at 3M, recounts a visit to his laboratory by the president of the company, the same William McKnight who later became chairman, when Appledorn was still a young scientist. McKnight dropped in and said, "Son, I hear you're doing something interesting. Tell me about it." Appledorn says that visit kept him motivated for nearly four decades. And it taught him how to motivate others.[18]

Laura Wills likewise recalled encouragement from Bob Russell, the president of Russell Branding, after creating her first successful Web design for a client. Russell, recognizing her talent and drive, asked her to build the e-commerce business for his company. Ignited by the personal vote of confidence, Wills "went hell-bent into the job." Within a year she had won an award for Web site design from the Canadian Advertising Council, and e-commerce was on its way to growing into almost half of the firm's work.

In both these cases, an individual performer got a life-changing boost from a leader's personal encouragement. That boost radiated excellence into the company far beyond the individual.

Excellent performers thrive on audience appreciation. They also need support when they experience losses. Susan Sacks, a sales director at Steelcase, relates a story about how her company responded when one corporate experiment returned poor results. Steelcase had recently bought IDEO, one of the world's largest and most creative industrial design firms. "Our idea was to leave IDEO and the culture that makes them so creative alone and send Steelcase employees on nine-month missions to Palo Alto to work in the IDEO environment, bring back what they learned, and seed our insular environment in Grand Rapids."[19] Whereas cultural change at Steelcase was not an immediate result, Steelcase leaders saw the experience as a valuable first experiment. The employees received appreciative recognition for advancing the long-term creative effort. They then were debriefed and participated in distilling lessons for the next wave of employees to take into the next cycle with IDEO. That next cycle of the experiment produced better results, and the first employees felt, rightly, part of those good results. The message communicated was that creative work involves moving through failures.

The Town Crier

Leaders intent on changing an entire company into a systemically creative community might think about the town criers of historic Europe. According to historian Isabel V. Hull, the criers' dissemination of information and the discussions that the news provoked led people to coalesce into communities of opinion that then influenced the larger society.[20]

The same thing happens in the smaller society of a company. According to business historian Stuart Crainer, though the common myth is that people change organizations, it is more often organizations that transform the perspectives, aspirations, and behavior of people.[21] Leaders who disseminate information with care, commitment, and clear intent can transform the expectations, opinions, and, eventually, the creative climate of a company.

When 3M announces that it expects to become the world's most innovative company, the message is sent to the international media and into 3M's own internal community. Awards announcements on its Web site include the names of the inventors and teams involved, reinforcing the message. Banners announcing the birth of new inventions are hung throughout the company. The importance of innovation is reinforced in the minds and hearts of every employee daily. The barrage of communication feeds a developing dialogue about creativity. Employees become familiar with the topic, communities of opinion form on how to make it happen, and creativity becomes a systemic part of the company's culture.

Newsletters at Tufts Health Care Plan and Steelcase spread the word about in-house innovative efforts and successes, contributing to the overall atmosphere of innovation and pointing staff to technologies and markets ready for further development. At Steelcase, where the learning curve about creativity was steep, learning has remained a focus in the creative climate. So leaders promote stories that, like the IDEO experiments, are weighted toward learning. These stories, like parables from the Bible, illustrate values that have made the company unique and keep them fresh.

Company lore at 3M centers on mavericks and their successes and failures. As one anecdote goes, for example, Lew Lehr, a young product developer, was convinced of the potential of surgical drapes even as the business was failing in the marketplace. Told to drop the project, he agreed to kill it as soon as inventory was used up—then neglected to tell the factory to stop producing the drapes until there was sufficient inventory to try several more markets. One of those efforts led to a contract with the U.S. military, and a second chance. Lehr developed the surgical drape business into what is now a $2 billion line of health-care products. The story of Lehr's stubbornness is widely circulated by company leaders as inspiration and instruction. And the moral of the story is that leaders who become or send "town criers" for creativity through their company will see the community coalesce around values important to that creativity.

Challenges

Leaders who challenge employees with ambitious creative goals can inspire employees to accomplish and sometimes exceed the goals. Leaders at General Motors, for example, challenged the employees who built the first Saturn car to reinvent the automobile. Ultimately they came up with a new way for GM to build cars and part of the industry was recalibrated. In 1993, leaders at 3M challenged everybody in the company to produce 30 percent of revenues from products created in the past four years. The challenge was met in three years. Tufts Health Care Plan delegates responsibility as a challenge to creativity. To communicate the message about independent creative initiative, Steve Leichtman tells THCP teams, "'We hired you for your creativity and intelligence. You know as much as we do and maybe more. Use it.' And they do."

Challenges like these—open, flexible, aggressive—arouse the competitive instincts of ambitious employees and release their creative energy. They increase the odds that you will tap the intrinsic motivation and curiosity and ignite the imagination and drive of the employees without evoking the fear of failure or of violating standard procedures.

Encourage creative performers, set up a "town crier," challenge employees' creativity. Company leaders who do these things will communicate loudly and clearly that the company values creativity. This confirmation of new expectations will elicit creative behavior and speed the change to systemic creativity.

Resources

As with any other initiative, leaders need to provide resources to instill systemic creativity. Some of them will be tangible, such as physical resources and training. Many involve such intangibles as goal setting, feedback, and diversity. The intangibles are no less a resource and no less important than the tangibles. To the extent that leaders do provide them, especially in their most effective form, intangible resources will contribute to systemic creativity as much as or more than tangible resources.

Goal Setting

Leaders who include creativity in a company's explicit vision or goals make creativity a priority for every employee. Leaders who then expect employees to take responsibility for setting and achieving local creativity goals for themselves help employees assume hands-on participation in the change to creativity. Leaders who expect employees to participate in setting goals for the entire business give employees the deepest intrinsic motivation to creatively further the goals.[22]

Many companies in recent years have widened corporate goals beyond financial growth to include values (customer satisfaction), ambition (to be the preferred supplier), direction (moving from health maintenance to total health care), and creativity (achieving 30 percent of revenue from recent products). In his book *The Balanced Scorecard,* business theorist Robert Kaplan recommends four goal categories: financial goals, customer expectations, internal business processes, and learning and growth. The learning and growth goal, ensuring that a company can sustain its ability to change and improve, is in large part a creativity goal. Kaplan suggests that financial goals may be the most important, but he stresses that failure to meet any of the goals will weaken the organization.[23]

Leaders will better ensure that creativity is taken to heart by giving employees the opportunity and responsibility to set goals of their own. For example, Tufts Health Care Plan has an explicit corporate goal of creativity, backed up by a figure-it-out-yourself ethos that expects creativity from every employee. Chairman Harris Berman challenged the company to "reach a million members by 2001," and then he gave teams the opportunity to work out their own goals, criteria for success, plan for problem solving, and eventual solution. Employees directed their own creativity and collectively met the challenge two years ahead of schedule.

Psychologist Abraham Maslow says, "It is well to treat working people as if they were high type Theory Y human beings, not only because of the Golden Rule, and not only because of the Declaration of Independence, and not only because of the Bible or some religious precept or anything like that, but also because this is the path to success of any kind whatsoever, including financial success."[24] Appropriately placed and oriented and given room to build their own goals into corporate goals, employees will bring creative flexibility and fresh ideas to bear on their work. Leaders who make creativity a corporate goal and then allow employees to engage with the creative process by setting their own goals are reinforcing the company's commitment to systemic creativity even as they infuse it both from the top down and from the bottom up.

Feedback

Leaders who build sensitive feedback mechanisms provide an important resource to the company that wants to be creative. All employees need feedback and need it presented in a balanced manner. Feedback to employees regarding their creative work, however, presents a singular challenge. Much research, including work done by Harvard's Teresa Amabile, contends that threatening or controlling evaluation of creative work undermines creativity.[25]

One way to minimize undermining creativity is to encourage employees to gather information about their performance themselves and then evaluate the performance themselves. Feedback from people who have mutual goals, like supervisors and colleagues, is also important to individual assessment. How this feedback is structured can strongly influence creative performance. For example, focusing on how to improve gets better results than focusing on what went wrong. And, as in the case of conflict, staying away from the personal and focusing clearly on operations and strategy is important to creatively hearing and adjusting as a result of feedback. Peer-to-peer feedback can be useful because peers know the multiple pressures facing the individual under review and can recognize in detail how the individual has negotiated these pressures.

All-around feedback, or 360-degree feedback, can be effective in a creative climate, especially when it remains constructive and emphasizes strengths, intrinsic motivation, skill levels, and advancement toward goals. Pete Karolczak set this kind of feedback as a norm at the inception of the new software division he started for Hewlett-Packard. In Karolczak's unit, 360-degree feedback meant that feedback went up and down the hierarchy and across from peer to peer at each level. This system gives an opportunity for superior-to-subordinate feedback and vice-versa, which reduces the hierarchical command and control that can inhibit creativity. It also gives employees a bigger pool of information from which to draw their own judgments about their performance.

Supervisors should give clear assessments of each individual's challenges and performance, but it is important to recognize that fear influences how people receive assessment. Even when reviewers try to be positive or simply fair in their assessment, some employees hear only criticism and discount the compliments. The unintended effect is to inhibit future creativity.

If you are the reviewer, you might get past this issue by asking employees to examine their own performances—from their own perspective as well as yours. Encourage employees to begin by outlining their personal goals and then evaluate how well they are meeting them. In discussing performance, cover areas of strength before areas that need improvement, as strengths often get missed, especially when employees are defensive and themselves focus on faults. Most employees in an environment of genuine openness are right on the mark in their self-assessments and can turn the assessments to productive use. Leaders who use creatively effective feedback as a resource can keep creative employees on course and simultaneously reinforce progress toward systemic creativity.

Providing for Diversity

As leaders inculcate creativity in their company, they experience many types of creative temperament. Diversity of temperament can be a resource. As we have said, a company's creativity is best served when the company supports the broadest possible spectrum of individual approaches and thinking.

Some employees create well under competitive stress. Cooperation stimulates other individuals creatively. Some people create quietly and uncertainly, ultimately emerging from exploration with insightful and even groundbreaking ideas. Still others are decisive, rapid-fire creative thinkers.

Creative people who are competitive and decisive often thrive in traditional hierarchies by winning attention for their ideas. Plenty of effective creative thinkers, however, do not thrive within a traditional hierarchy. Their valuable creative contributions can easily be lost to the company and to themselves. The company first loses the perspectives brought by noncompetitive creative profiles and then in time loses the value of sensitive, reflective sensibilities.

Leaders who are aware of the natural tendency to select against diversity of types have a number of ways to see that the company recognizes and gets the benefit of every creative sensibility. Leaders at Guidant provide entrepreneurial leadership seminars, which include training in recognizing the diverse thinking styles of the company's employees. Hallmark has an office of innovation with a staff trained to appreciate many styles of creative thinking and to encourage all employees with promising ideas.[26] Bill Dunn, a manager at Baxter Healthcare, has created an Internet-based suggestion system in which every employee immediately receives $20 on submitting an idea. Their ideas are kept, with their names and with keywords denoting the type of idea, in an active "innovation holding area" and brought up whenever innovation of that type is under consideration. If an employee's idea generates active attention, he or she is invited to participate in the idea's development.[27]

Leaders at 3M encourage diversity by providing two equivalent career paths for creative workers. Employees can either become business managers or continue working in the laboratory and advancing to the position of corporate scientist. These two paths let people who are more creative in the reflective climate of research than in the management ranks rise in the company while remaining in a climate that nourishes their creative temperament.

The creative process thrives on diversity. A creative company needs policies and practices to secure all possible diversity of creative types among the company's employees and leadership.

Training

Most business managers, with or without an M.B.A., have not studied creativity or how to build a creative culture or how to work with teams creatively. Companies can readily provide training in these areas.

Russell provides creative problem-solving training to all staff. The entire top management team at Tufts Health Care Plan takes training in both problem solving and creativity. Guidant helps employees understand elements of personal importance, covering how they understand their relationship to their world, what is personally important, and how and when to start the conversations that affect their world. The second course of training covers how to bring creativity to bear on these topics. The former Compaq had several people on staff who researched, designed, and led in-house creativity seminars. Lucent and the Certainteed Corporation both have full-time staff who research creativity methods as well as train in them. The Walt Disney Company provides classes that cover creative thinking, management of creativity, and application of those skills across the art forms.

Training works. Studies show that creativity training and creative problem-solving training lead to higher scores on creative thinking tests and to subsequent business results.[28] After creativity courses, skills like divergent thinking, tolerance of ambiguity, use of multiple perspectives, and creation of more numerous ideas can improve dramatically: Some participants score dramatically higher on tests of creative abilities after training. As we described in chapter 4, Frito-Lay and Sysco have both had dramatic success with creativity training.

Training is an available, sensible resource. Provide it, and you will see improved productivity flowing from a stronger creative climate.

Physical Resources

Studies show that creativity and purposeful innovation increase when leaders can make more money, material, time, staff, and space available. Employees view extra resources as an indication of relaxed control, which in itself stimulates creativity. Extra resources also give innovative projects of higher risk a better chance of being approved, as there is more room to experiment and to pilot and improve concepts before a decision has to be made.

The relationship between resources and innovation is curvilinear. In other words, with too few resources, innovation atrophies, and with too many resources, discipline and focus tend to suffer. At the highest point of the curve, one study found the level of innovative results reaches four times what it is when companies run lean and efficient. Studies have not found a single optimal point of excess resources, however, noting only that a greater degree of added resources may work better in growing industries than in shrinking ones—although some amount of added resources works in both.[29]

The optimal blend of physical resources differs from company to company and situation to situation. But many companies can benefit from experiments in generosity, since most of them have already experimented with cost reduction.

Computer memory systems executive Ray Miller saw a striking difference after his technical unit was sold to Hyundai:

Under our previous owner, we submitted our business plan annually and went through a back-and-forth process to justify each budget item. This year, under Hyundai, we submitted our business plan as usual, but managers came back to us with only one question: "If we were to give you a 50 percent increase in your budget, how would you use it?" What a change in attitude! The ideas we came up with were astounding.[30]

A 50 percent budget increase sounds too good to be true, but the 15 percent time given to all employees for personal projects by 3M and the 30 percent renewal time and budget offered by Hallmark are useful models for any leader.

When you can give additional resources to creativity, you allow for more experiments and your overall risk can decrease.

Guiding the Corporation

Reduced controls, creativity-friendly rewards, new attitudes about efficiency and failure, productive messages about creative change, and added resources are all important in fostering creativity. But simply providing the ingredients is not enough. Company leaders intent on a systemically creative organization must consciously and continuously guide the entire fabric of the change into a creative process and the climate that allows and empowers it.

Guiding the systemically creative company has three areas of responsibility: watching (monitor and understand), acting (initiate change, build a coalition, plan, and experiment), and learning (gather feedback, capture lessons, and add to the body of understanding). Watching, acting, and learning take place in a constantly continuing cycle.

Watching (Monitor and Understand)

Start by identifying and defining the existing climate in the company. Assessment tools are a useful first step. Tools differ in how they gauge a climate's ability to support creativity and innovation, but they can develop a detailed picture that people can agree is valid.[31]

Periodic surveys can provide important indicators of progress. Questions for employees might cover personal perception of safety, fear of failure, autonomy, degree of interest in and satisfaction from work, ease of access to diverse information, level of challenge in individual jobs, frequency of new ideas, perception of effectiveness of the new ideas, support from management and colleagues, availability of resources, major barriers and aids to success, and effectiveness of teams or coalitions.

Surveys and questionnaires and any other diagnostics lead to a growing and increasingly sophisticated understanding about the company and its climate and about how creativity and innovation play out across the company. This understanding will help ensure that early experiments in the change to creativity take hold.

Acting (Initiate Change, Build a Coalition, Plan, and Experiment)

Guiding a systemically creative company involves action in three stages.

1. Initiate Change   Any effort to instill creativity across a company requires an unusual effort to change momentum. This effort should harness both the attraction of a vision and the compulsion of a need to change.[32]

In terms of vision, "The leader has to provide the hook," says Susan Adam, a director at Publishers Clearing House, "and the hook has to be personal for every individual. Take, for example, Martin Luther King's 'I have a dream' speech. Everyone related to that dream personally and could work toward achieving it in his own creative way."[33]

Sometimes, however, a change program is a matter of survival. "At Publishers Clearing House," says Todd Sloane, another director, "there is a direct relationship between how creative we are and how many people respond to our offerings. If we cannot continue to keep their interest in fresh ways sales will decline."[34]

Visions vary widely: 3M aims to be the most innovative company in the world; Tufts Health Care Plan intends to be the fastest-growing health-care institution in New England; Guidant wants to remain solidly entrepreneurial. Crisis situations also differ: Tufts Health Care Plan had to compete with health-care providers two or three times its size; the software division at Hewlett-Packard had to deal with an industry changing so rapidly that every six months a new paradigm emerged.

According to a director at a national bank during the mid-1990s, "We had two reasons that convinced others to let us invest in a more creative division. First, we were on a burning platform, in this case from the advent of e-commerce. There was no question that our bank would sink into obscurity unless we adopted a fundamentally different way of doing business." Second, the director said, division leaders had a vision, a "future pull," when, at a meeting called by their CEO they were asked to "virtually resign from the bank" in order to distance themselves from their old, set thinking and redesign the bank for the future. The group worked for several days, creating a brand-new bank piecemeal and then integrating the parts into a compelling whole. From the director's perspective, both the push from the burning platform and the pull from the future vision were critical. "People need more than just something good to go to; they have to see something bad behind them."

2. Build a Coalition   Some companies appoint an individual to head an innovation change. We have found that the multiple perspectives of a coalition, team, or steering committee can be more successful. The coalition, assembled to gather and interpret the information that sets the initial course for a more creative future, should include people at the top of the organization. But leaders with positional power need to resist the urge to mandate the changes that make a more creative organization; in fact, the

more they try to do so, the more they will kill the free and supportive climate required for sustained innovation.

The coalition must also include individuals who have gained
the ear of significant portions of the organization through experience, talent, and character. Some of these people may have a better rapport with management, others with employees, still others
with market analysts. A successful coalition grows as more people in the company embrace a creative organization. As the company begins to introduce innovations to the outside world, the
coalition can reach vendors and customers. Eventually the size of
the coalition should reach a critical mass capable of sustaining the
new order across the organization.

3. Plan and Experiment   Plan the change to creativity continuously and flexibly. Allow for unplanned experiments, and
adjust your plan as experiments bring surprising results. Creativity is not predictability. Planning for uncertainty helps employees
and organizations be prepared for numerous scenarios, including
occasional failure. Adjusting the plan as necessary and continuing
to plan keep the planning relevant and keep the change to creativity going forward. As much as possible, for as long as possible,
keep creativity planning separate from fiscal planning, or the
creativity planning will suffer from the pressures of short-term,
bottom-line contingencies.

Learning (Gather Feedback, Capture Lessons, and Add to the Body of Understanding)

As the change to systemic creativity advances, effective, guiding leadership will make a point of learning from every earlier
step. Without a conscious effort to learn, when projects go awry
and are shut down there will be no positive issue from the effort,
no increased grasp of the creative process in context. And if corporate priorities change without formalized institutional learning,
a whole change program can die—and all creative momentum
along with it.

Gather the feedback from creative experiments and extract the lessons offered about the change to creativity and its mechanics in your company. Capturing these lessons will make success in future experiments and projects more likely. It will also add to the body of understanding about creativity in your company, which will give the company the ongoing knowledge and confidence critical to continuing creative evolution.

SEVEN

Purposeful Creativity

B Y "PURPOSEFUL CREATIVITY," we mean creativity applied to specific issues. "Innovation" is, in our terminology,
the result, the change in the order of things, the solution that
comes from the work of purposeful creativity.

In our research—and in the thousands of innovation-focused
interactions Synectics has conducted with individuals, groups, and
organizations over the past forty years—we identified seven stages
in the purposeful creativity that generates successful innovation:
groundwork and immersion; divergent exploration; selection; focused exploration; initial articulation of a potential solution; development and transformation; and implementation. Although
they are not definitive or exclusive, the seven stages embody much
of what is currently known about creative thinking. Within each
of the seven stages, a variety of tools boosts freshness of thinking
and facilitates success. The stages have been used across the full
spectrum of business challenges in multiple industries to help
banks develop new products, high-technology companies create
new business models, pharmaceutical companies devise research

programs, and entrepreneurs create new businesses. Many professional creators have discovered similar progressions for use in domains from art to science to industry.

People learn new techniques more quickly when they actually apply them to a problem. So, at Synectics training sessions, participants work on real issues that affect their job or their organization. In that spirit, we offer examples from work with two companies, Citibank and Nabisco, as well as with an individual at the Museum of Science, Boston. Citibank was addressing an issue that many companies faced. Nabisco was creating new products. And David Rabkin, a vice president with responsibility for new technology-related exhibits and programs at the museum, needed to bring creativity to his day-to-day responsibilities.

Stage 1: Groundwork and Immersion

Begin the course toward an innovative solution with a strategic appraisal and the groundwork and immersion appropriate to the scope and matter of the problem or opportunity at hand. For purposeful creativity, assess a problem and potential methods for solving it before diving into problem solving. Ask yourself what you know about the problem and what you might need to know. Immerse yourself in the information you gather. The more you know about a problem and its context, the greater the chance for an effective solution. This is the same "rich in, rich out" approach that professional strategists practice. Creative strategists draw on an even broader array of information because creative solutions often exist well beyond the scope of anything previously considered.

Jackie Burton, the Citibank executive in charge of strategy dealing with the Y2K computer crisis that loomed in the1990s, constructed a diverse team of experts including systems designers, technical researchers, and business strategists from the bank itself. He also included an MIT programmer, a theorist in the fledgling field of knowledge management, and the technical editor of

Science News, who was familiar with every publicly known emerging technology. With this scope of expertise, the group was able to consider the problem broadly and deeply.[1]

While deep immersion is valuable, it involves a risk. Strong analysis uses an assumed framework that can inadvertently limit exploration to that very framework and defeat creativity. Ken Olsen, the brilliant founding president of Digital Equipment Corporation, ran into this limitation in the 1970s when, using the very soundest assumptions of the time, he conducted an analysis to discover how to serve the future of his industry. One of the assumptions underlying his analysis was that there would not be a market for home computing.[2] So that eventuality was never fully explored. Companies including Nabisco, Deutsche Bank, KPMG, and Steelcase, on the other hand, have developed new and reliable insights by offering strategic groups lots of information but requiring less rigid analysis, as free from assumption as possible. They then encourage members of the groups to remain open to a broad array of possible circumstances and form their own opinions about strategic possibilities and solutions.

Using this hybrid, analytical/serendipitous approach, Jim Keene, when he was director of strategy at Steelcase, provided a broad range of information when he kicked off the annual planning process in 1999 with a "Fact Pack." Three quarters of his "Fact Pack" was devoted to the external world, including "information on the economy, cultural diversity, white- and blue-collar issues, our customers, the Silicon Valley shift, what the management gurus were saying, virtual teams, personal productivity issues, workplace space, and the American culture."[3] Only the fourth quarter of his "Fact Pack" covered internal factors such as goals, strengths, weaknesses, and performance indicators. Keene immersed the planning group in this eclectic mix of information before planning started in earnest because he wanted "the unexpected as well as the usual, even if it makes people uncomfortable. This information provoked deeper questioning that led to better ideas."

To begin purposeful creativity, groups need a disconnecting agent between the restricting criteria of analysis and the creative search for a solution. Part of the groundwork is considering which approaches will deliver the most creatively useful understanding of a problem and lead to its eventual solution: an analytical approach, a research approach, or a creative approach. Even when an approach has worked before, will the same approach effectively describe the current problem? Should the approach be modified? Are there ways to make it better? These questions increase the chances of posing and then attacking the problem in the way that's most likely to yield an eventual creative solution.

When Nabisco wanted to create a broad pipeline of product concepts for research and development, Wayne Puglia, the project head, knew the company was looking three to five years out or more. In their planning, Puglia's group first had to catalog where they were rich and where they were sparse in ideas so that they could direct the exploration accordingly. Then they considered which information might be useful when the thinking started in earnest. They looked at their own technical research and that of their affiliates for promising technologies, for strategically proprietary strengths, and for underutilized capacity.[4] Then they broadened the focus to the markets they serve. Recognizing that current customer information would not work well for three years out, they hired in-house and outside trend experts to provide glimpses into the future that might spark useful idea generation.

They also designed the process the group would use. Puglia knew that people from R&D, marketing, and strategy would be needed in many different product areas if the products conceived were to fit Nabisco's markets, strategies, and capabilities. So he divided the conception of product ideas into segments, each segment focusing on a strategically important area of market growth. And in anticipation of a wealth of ideas, the group decided that ideas would have to be sorted and a strategy set for moving ahead, probably with a new mix of people, after the conception process. This thinking and work occurred weeks and months before the actual work of conceiving product ideas began.

At Boston's Museum of Science, David Rabkin had been thinking about "how to design the experience we want our visitors to have with technology."[5] Like most people, Rabkin had unconsciously formed ways to get new ideas, and he'd used them to get some ideas about designing the museum's experience. When we asked him to be explicit about what actions or thinking had helped him come up with these ideas, Rabkin concluded that he was unconsciously "putting myself in the mind of different audience members, changing my assumptions, or exaggerating what I hope can be done and then asking what that would mean."

Other clients of whom we asked the same questions reported using a variety of tactics to get ideas—creating mental imagery, recalling what others have done in similar situations, changing their focus by going for a walk. These tactics to get new ideas are often so habitual or so taken for granted that people don't notice them. But to improve the ability to get new ideas, people need to gauge the relative worth of their own ideas and then identify the way they got the best ones.

We asked Rabkin to list some of the ideas he had been considering and rate each for "newness" on a scale of 1 to 9, with 1 being, "predictable" and 9 "surprising." This rating criterion is thoroughly subjective. Newness is only one aspect of a good creative idea—others are appropriateness to task, flexibility of application, qualities of insight, aesthetics, and truth. The rating process gives you practice assessing your own creative thought and in each case thinking about it in terms that lead toward exploration. Rabkin found that his first three ideas followed common and very predictable themes for him, "the kind of work I've done for years." The sixth idea, persuading visitors to view technology from the perspectives of artists, journalists, and activists, was the most surprising for him, but he still rated it only "4" for newness.

Creativity Tool: Immersion for Insight

Immersion in new information is one way to set aside old assumptions to help ensure that the statement of a problem is deeply connected to real needs. We recommend that you spend time with customers and meet with people outside your industry who face challenges somewhat similar to yours. If you are an equipment manufacturer experiencing a limit to your growth, meet with people from equipment companies in another industry, possibly companies that grew by moving from selling products to selling solutions. Listen to their stories.

An insurance company used this tool when it was rethinking a product that consumers resisted buying. To approach the problem, it first gathered consumers to talk about insurance generally and the problem type of insurance specifically. At points during the interview process, the moderator used metaphorical questions to get a better understanding of the minds of the consumers and to uncover their emotional responses to the problem. One of the questions that proved pivotal was "If insurance were a weather pattern, what pattern would it be?" One consumer answered, "A blizzard, because it inundates me with a storm of paperwork." There were many different responses to this question, but the "blizzard" answer led company executives to understand that the problem was not just about consumer attitudes toward the insurance industry and the product under consideration but also about threat—that the customer didn't trust the insurance companies. The executives stayed open and considered this distrust, ultimately recognizing that they themselves had triggered it. Their company had treated the customers with distrust first, by making the customers sign a "blizzard" of voluminous and detailed contracts full of legal language. This insight led the company to build an improved way of going to market, a new way of executing contracts, and finally better customer service to support a much improved product.

Additional Considerations for Group Groundwork

Groups that undertake a purposeful creative effort need to do strategic groundwork, including determining who will participate, what roles the participants will play, and how much time to allocate to the work. Groups work best when at least one and usually more of the participants specifically own responsibility for the development and implementation of a solution. We call this person(s) the problem owner, the person who will leave the meeting and do something with the results. The group also increases its effectiveness by including other people who have a stake in the problem. And beyond that, the broader the range of perspective and expertise in the group, the better the chances of reaching a solution.

Include people who are not enmeshed in the problem for new ways of looking at the problem. Nabisco, for example, included scientists, strategists, market researchers, and even a visual artist who drew rather than verbalized his ideas. This diversity in the group led product managers, who were deeply knowledgeable about the problem, to broader perspectives that they could then shape into solutions.

Creativity groups also benefit from designating one person to act as a facilitator, to guide the thinking process and interaction within the group. People are not usually skilled at creating collectively or at maintaining a supportive climate for creativity. Even people with good experience in working collaboratively have different opinions about the best approach to any given task. Anxieties about working together diminish a group's ability to think creatively. Or group members with hierarchical authority may try to settle arguments arbitrarily, closing off further creative exploration. A facilitator without rank or a stake in the outcome can ameliorate procedural contentions without arousing resistance and leave the group free to turn its full attention to exploring new ideas and solutions.

Finally, give the group time for blind alleys. A day and a half of solid creative work before coming to a solution is preferable to a single day's work, two and a half days are even better than that, and multiple sessions are best. It often takes a group a full day to warm up enough to genuinely begin new exploration. The downtime of an overnight break recharges a group's energy, making people more productive the second day. And having slept on the problem, people often find surprisingly fresh directions in the morning. And finally, when there is time to make mistakes, people are more willing to take risks with experimental—and potentially breakthrough—thinking.

For Groundwork and Immersion

- Determine what information will help you without boxing you in.
- Consider involving other people whose thoughts might be valuable.
- Organize the progress of your thinking to get from sometimes obscure problems to clear solutions and implementation.
- Get perspective from people, including customers, outside the company.

Stage 2: Divergent Exploration

In the second stage of purposeful creativity, you attack the entirety of a problem from every angle by creating as many and various directions of exploration as possible. Consider a wide spectrum of approaches, without becoming stymied by problems or details. For successful creative problem solving, avoid rushing to one solution and/or discarding other potentially viable possibilities too quickly. Surveying a rich array of initial possibilities, you might first identify the most interesting possibilities individually, then in combination with each other. Then begin to focus on the details.

The divergent exploration stage creates many doorways, each of which represents a different approach to a solution. Behind each doorway is a workroom with a different set of givens the problem solver can work with to fashion the necessary solution. The more doorways you create, the greater the possibility of unimagined and perhaps better solutions.

There are several tools with which you can activate divergent exploration and develop the largest and most varied possible list of approaches to a problem.

Creativity Tool: Wishing

Most adults can remember how to suspend disbelief when they begin to think about solutions to their problems using the words "I wish . . . ." We have found that when people and groups wish at the beginning of the purposeful creative thinking effort, two things happen: First, the wishes grow fresher, larger and more fanciful, and second, they come closer and closer to what the thinker really wants to happen. Wishing engages intrinsic motivation.

In one effort, the new product development group at Nabisco wished for packaging that enriches the eating experience and for foods that take calories away as people eat them. The impossible is as easy to wish for as the plausible, since nobody has to worry about making the wishes come true, at least not at the outset.

Wishing also reveals new layers of a problem, and with that comes the understanding that a solution will need to be multifaceted. Equally important, wishing often reveals unarticulated or hidden motives and desires of the problem solver. When David Rabkin began wishing about new ways to design the visitor experience at the Museum of Science, he found that two things happened. "I became more outrageous as I went along. And the wishes had a lot more to do with me, with why I really care about what I'm doing." For example, one of his wishes was "I wish the museum could make learning as thrilling as bungee jumping." In this wish, Rabkin blended a personal motivation—to instill in others the thrill of learning—with the museum's need for a strong visitor experience. This wish helped him to infuse more of his creative energy into his problem solving.

Groups that use wishing usually become more deeply engaged with the challenge. When each member states his or her wish and reveals some of what is intrinsically important, everyone's unique expertise and experience become more available for the creative process, and the group's collective thinking expands to include the motivations and desires expressed. As this happens, the group bonds more deeply and creatively around the common goal of creative problem solving.

Creativity Tool: Overcoming False Fatigue

The divergent explorations in Stage 2 are useful not only for the variety of approaches created, but also for the richness and freshness that comes from stretching for multiple possibilities. The person who is willing to propose more and more options in dealing with his or her problem is doing something important—pushing past the point when all the predictable solutions have been proposed past the point of stretching until silliness kicks in, and past the point of "false fatigue" into unpredictable realms of effort where new and creative thought of the highest quality is most likely.

To teach creativity, Lowry Burgess, professor of art and dean at Carnegie Mellon University, asks his students to make two hundred two-foot by four-foot drawings in two weeks. One of his students, an author of this book, at first gathered together various interesting objects for a still life and spent a couple of hours drawing his best rendition. He then set up another still life. By the end of the day he had only five drawings, so he began to draw faster. Soon he was doing outlines and impressions and then just drawn gestures of the same still life. After about ninety drawings, the works resembled children's scribbles. After a hundred and fifty drawings, the student became bored with the scribbles and laid six two-by-four sheets on the ground outside and ran over them with his motorcycle, making track drawings. This prompted him to go up to the roof and dribble paint onto six more sheets from two stories above. Creating drawings in sixes became fun and new territory for the student. So he went back inside, taped one sheet to a wall, crumpled five others, pasted them onto the first, and called the whole thing, "3D Drawings, Six Perspectives."[6]

This student's experience is not atypical in the course of purposeful creative thinking. Often a problem solver's most creative thoughts appear only after he or she has first wrung out their mind. As was the case with David Rabkin, initial ideas about a problem tend to be usual thinking. After exhausting those ideas, people try to stretch. As they stretch more and more, their internal censoring mechanisms break down. Eventually, they reach the point of "false fatigue" where they suppose they have generated all the ideas they can. At this point, to produce more ideas, they have to loosen up to go beyond the point where risking new thoughts feels threatening. And then they start to surprise themselves. The harder the problem, the more useful this approach is. Citibank, in tackling the Y2K problem, had already examined and exhausted all known approaches. In the effort to find more approaches, the team wished for six hours straight, overcame the false fatigue, and generated 180 new approaches, ranging from the intriguing and potentially useful to the absurd.

Creativity Tool: Changing Perspectives with Metaphor

Using metaphors helps people expand the divergent exploration stage of the purposeful creativity process by revealing previously invisible relationships. When the insurance company learned that customers experienced the company product as a "blizzard" inundating them with paperwork, company executives could understand the customers' frustration palpably. This understanding led to a successful product that did not come across as a blizzard.

A New York bank's development director, trying to anticipate how the bank would work with customers in ten years' time, began thinking of metaphors for the bank-customer relationship. Two he considered were "mother" and a 1950s television program, *Topper,* in which a ghost family helped out a man named Topper. Each metaphor suggested new roles for the bank in relation to its customers. In the "mother" metaphor, the bank was always in the customer's business, advising, helping, nurturing, always with the customer's best interest at heart. The television show metaphor, on the other hand, suggested that the bank be an invisible friend, there when wanted and gone when not. The ghosts, with their beer-guzzling St. Bernard, also had a sense of humor with Topper, which suggested to the development director that the bank might lightly tease the customer from time to time, adding personality to the relationship.

A pharmaceutical company generated useful metaphors by "taking pictures of the problem." Trying to restructure the company's HR department, the team kept getting mired in a limited number of options. So each person got a Polaroid camera and went off to take pictures that captured the idea of a "complicated organization." One person returned with a picture of a small carnival, complete with rides, food stands, and community booths. Reflecting on the picture and the organization of the carnival, this particular team member observed how entirely different constituents meshed together to make one whole with little apparent central direction. This observation led him to suggest reducing the current HR department to just a few people and replacing the rest of the fifty-person department with representatives, different constituents, from other departments. In this concept, the representatives would retain their connection to their original departments and take on HR as a partial responsibility.

Creativity Tool: Focusing Creative Thought with Analogy

Creating an analogy is useful in divergent exploration. Look at two unrelated things—one thing from the problem and something from an unrelated world. Find the relation between them, and tease from the comparison a new idea. Analogy often goes to the heart of the problem. When Doug Farmer thought about what the "flow" in traffic had to do with the problem of oil flow in a refining operation, he was applying use of analogy to get outside his problem to find a fresh perspective. When social theorists use the term "global village," they are creating an analogy to suggest anew the relationship between the world and its once isolated communities caused by advances in communication. This understanding leads to innumerable ideas, inventions, and policies.

Analogies are more complicated to build than metaphors, but they're well worth trying. First find similarities between two unrelated things. Then interpret the comparison for meaning and milk it for new ideas.

During this phase of his work, we asked David Rabkin to select one random characteristic of his immediate surroundings. He pointed to the piles of paper on his desk. Analogies are easier to mine when they're rich with information, so we pushed Rabkin to think about the piles of paper in a broader sense. Rabkin said he thought about them as "part of the rat race." Exploring his experience of the rat race, Rabkin came up with this imagery: "house payments, obligations, long work hours, occasional recreation, being too tired to do anything but watch television."

Then with these experiences fresh in his mind, we had Rabkin refocus on his original problem: to design a powerful experience for the museum visitor. Holding the problem of the visitor's experience in his mind along with the analogy of the rat race, he looked for connections or similarities between the experiences. He then fashioned wishes from the connections for museum visitors: He wished that the museum could offer something to people who had no time at all. He wished he could reach people so tied into their jobs that they have no longer have outside interests.

As is the case with analogy, tools that enhance creativity often work counter to the mind's instinct to view a problem from a single perspective. Once a perspective is established, people have trouble thinking outside it. Creativity tools move people to fresh perspectives that provide new connections for new ideas. Using more tools brings problem solvers to more perspectives. This variety and richness increases the possibility of success in applying creativity to problems.

Excursion Methods

Many creative thinking methodologies follow a simple series of steps: Put the problem aside, even briefly; engage in thoughts that are full of imagery unrelated to the problem; bring the problem back to mind and find connections between the problem and the new images; then work those connections into a new thought that is relevant to solving the problem. The metaphor and analogy tools are forms of what Synectics calls "excursions." They are tools that can be used at any stage in the creative problem-solving approach.

Excursions work by placing the thinker in a new world that is seemingly irrelevant to the world of the problem and that consequently lacks the constraints inherent in the world of the problem. An excursion also removes the thinker from the fear and pressures associated with the problem, allowing higher curiosity to reach into experimental thought. The more irrelevant the imagery is to the real problem, the greater the potential for surprising connections and new ideas.

Alternatively, excursions can also involve physically changing a circumstance. One group, while trying to solve a problem, was interrupted by a fire alarm. They trudged down a stairway and outside, only to find that it was a false alarm. When they got back inside, the facilitator in the group asked each person to think about a conversation they had during the unexpected break and find a new idea hidden in it. Connections found this way or by analogy or metaphor may be serendipitously appropriate or seem completely obscure. What counts is for the mind to let go of the problem and fully enter the world of the new stimulus before attempting to search for connections and new ideas.

For Divergent Exploration   Allow yourself time and freedom to range widely in your thinking, in your wishing, in identifying any potential direction that could conceivably be of help; use creativity tools liberally whenever they might be useful.

Stage 3: Selection

After a multitude of possible approaches and infant ideas have been generated in the divergent exploration stage, the next step is to select the approaches likely to become or lead to the ideal solution. This selection stage determines how new and appealing the eventual solution will be. Begin with choosing a mix of possible approaches that, when pursued, will yield a solution that's comprehensive, feasible, exciting, and engaging.

A group generally has more difficulty than an individual with this process. Each person in the group has a different threshold for risk, and each person naturally uses a personal set of criteria in deciding what to explore. Groups often use more or less conscious criteria when selecting what is new, what is intriguing, and what is practical from the list of possibilities generated. Group voting tends to result in conservative selections because everyone can generally agree on what is important and feasible and thus practical, but not everyone agrees on what's new and intriguing. Consequently, the most practical selections almost always get the most votes.

To ensure newness, someone in the group with a high tolerance for risk has to urge the group through the more interesting doorways. This person could be the facilitator or the highest-ranking individual in the room or the person responsible for implementation. Or leadership can emerge from the most articulate person or be intentionally passed from person to person as different solutions come under consideration. In Citibank's Y2K session, for instance, the three most senior people decided in advance that they would focus only on the "most unusual" approaches to increase the possibility of new solutions.

Nabisco created hundreds of approaches in six days of work spanning two months and covering three strategic areas of potential growth in the marketplace. When it came time to select potential areas for further exploration, all participants in the working group had a chance to vote. But being aware that a large group's vote would tend to center on what was assumed to be most plausible, not on the fewer new and exciting ideas, Wayne Puglia created a small team within the group to ensure that creatively interesting approaches were not discarded. The team consisted of Puglia (himself from R&D) and one colleague each from marketing and corporate strategy. Together they intervened in the selection process to balance the selected approaches at 40 percent tactically important and short term and 50 percent creatively exciting and long term and potentially radical. For the remaining 10 percent they handed out "wild cards" to various members of the group who could then select any favorite and personally intriguing approach.

For David Rabkin, each wish held interest, but since he was looking for fresh ideas, he chose approaches that either intrigued him or that deviated radically from current practice in the museum's exhibits. At this stage he knew that he did not have to choose solutions that were possible or even specific. Consequently, among his selections for more exploration was "I wish our museum exhibits could make learning as thrilling as bungee jumping."

For Selection   Once you're satisfied that you have searched as thoroughly as possible for potentially interesting approaches to the problem, select from among these approaches, making a point not to overlook the really intriguing, the fundamentally different, or even the absurd approaches just because they seem impossible.

Stage 4: Focused Exploration

Once selections are made, consider one approach. Enter one "doorway" at a time and explore the approach with a maximum of creative effort.

This is not the time to judge. Many people think this is the time to evaluate, but evaluating wishes or approaches at this stage usually filters out all but the practical approaches, which is self-defeating. In Stage 4, balancing creativity and practicality is what matters most.

Beyond every doorway is what we call a "workshop" in which some wishes are fleshed out and some receive straightforward development. The pharmaceutical company, following up on the line of thought triggered by the photograph of a carnival, eventually did shrink HR to a five-person department with fifty part-time representatives from the line organization. However, they didn't do so until a cross-functional team spent a lot more time thinking through the idea, actively devising a plan, and finally obtaining corporatewide approval.

Out of its exhaustive approaches to its problem, Citibank ended up with eight possible solutions, ranging from software fixes to partnering options to bank restructuring. The bank simultaneously workshopped all eight potential solutions right up to the turn of the millennium.

For David Rabkin, the task was to convert his bungee jumping wish into more focused ideas about what kind of museum experience could be as thrilling as bungee jumping. Ideas that came immediately to mind included "helping people experience something they did not know was possible" and "demonstrating and explaining scientific magic."

This form of creative thinking, tightly focusing on a vague but stimulating wished-for solution, is often more difficult than generating the wish. Groups often do much better than individual creative thinkers at this stage simply because there are more people tackling the challenge; different perspectives trigger new thoughts in other members as they work.

One of the many wishful approaches that was selected by Nabisco because it was strategically attractive involved a candy called "Creme Savers." Not only was the candy already successful, but the swirl of fruit and cream on each piece was distinctive enough to have gained broad customer recognition. There was a wish to "expand on the success of both the candy and the swirl"; the group selected this wish as possibly having both strategic importance and creative interest. According to Wayne Puglia, the group felt that the idea had "huge potential. We could go almost anywhere with it."

In several workshops, the group then did in fact explore how the concept of Creme Savers and the icon of its swirl might lead to platforms for new growth beyond simple line extensions, might reach "beyond hard Life Saver sorts of candy to pudding and yogurt and softer candies." As Puglia said, "This group would have explored swirled floor tiles if we'd let them."

Creativity Tool: Images for Connection Making

At this stage, David Rabkin went on an excursion to expand his list of ideas about how to make the bungee jumping notion a reality. First, he thought about a movie he had seen, *My Cousin Vinny*. Invited to describe a favorite scene from it, Rabkin recalled the courtroom scene in which "Marisa Tomei displays her car expertise." Because the movie had established that Tomei worked in her father's garage and the only clue to a murder was an automobile, "the audience sees the set-up, knows the punch line is coming, and once they're ready, get it delivered perfectly." Now Rabkin spent time thinking about the scene, developing stronger, more detailed imagery, noticing any thread of connection to bungee jumping. Then, as part of the process, he had to use that connection to craft a potential solution for the problem of designing the museum's visitor experience. He saw a connection with how the set-up in the movie enhanced the delivery of the punch line. From that, he came up with the idea of "establishing a context in the mind of the museum visitor in advance of seeing an exhibit" so that visitors would fully appreciate the exhibit when they did see it. And after they saw it, "We need a way to prompt the viewer to reflect on their experience. All three parts—set-up, presentation, reflection—need to work together for the greatest impact." Thinking about the set-up in the movie (or the fear and excitement just before bungee jumping), Rabkin wondered how an exhibit might enter the homes of museum visitors before they came to the museum. Maybe a science puzzle could be mailed to visitors ahead of time, a puzzle that could be figured out only by finding a clue in the particular exhibit at the museum. Taking this idea further, Rabkin speculated that the museum might produce Internet-capable videos that could be either sent on disks or downloaded from the museum's Web site.

This connection-making tool about movies uses the same procedure as the metaphor and analogy excursions: forget the problem, generate unrelated material, find a connection between problem and material, and draw an idea from the connection. The movie had no relation either to bungee jumping or to the Museum of Science. The movie memories simply revived a complex of imagery and meaning in Rabkin's consciousness, and this complex presented Rabkin with potential subjective points of connection, however obscure, to the wished-for bungee jumping. His creative mind seized on some of the points to synthesize new ideas that might become his solution.

Creativity Tool: Using Outside Stimuli

During all the Nabisco new-product sessions, Harvey Ehrlich, a visual artist, sat at the back generating ideas with the group.[7] By plan, Ehrlich never said a word; instead he drew his ideas in full color—packages, candies, advertising ideas, whatever came to mind as a result of the activity in the room. At several points during each session, all conversation stopped, and the group gathered around Ehrlich to talk about the visuals, to draw stimulation to connections and ideas. The process sparked additional new thoughts, including the idea that the iconic Nabisco trademarks could carry new imagery, like stars and people and text; that they could even become three-dimensional. New exploration sprang from each of these new directions. One resulting idea that came to market in 2002 was Creme Savers yogurt, based on the swirl and flavors of Nabisco's successful Creme Savers candies.

Creativity Tool: Fast Connection Making

Many creativity tools such as the one that follows can be deployed quite quickly, allowing the creator to repeat them frequently throughout the process. We asked David Rabkin to turn to any page of a magazine and search it for five new ideas that would help realize his wish for visitors to experience the Museum of Science like bungee jumping. He quickly found five, one of which was "Looking at a picture of a ship washed up on the rocks, I wondered how the problem of saving the ship would be solved, which made me think that there was something we could do with solving impossible puzzles through science. How could you ever figure out how to save this ship?" Suddenly an idea crystallized for Rabkin. "Science has found ways to deal with each situation. We want to get people to think first how they would work on a problem like this ship on the rocks, fully engage their minds on it. Then we can lead them to the scientific tools available and help them think up a better answer."

Excursion tools used with a group of ten people often result in dozens to hundreds of fresh ideas because each person in the group uses different stimuli on a different store of personal experience; in making their ideas public, they trigger even more thoughts in other members of the group.

The particular value of fast connection making is that the pressure to respond quickly bypasses self-censoring and so allows new ideas to emerge with all their originality. It's best to use this tool after building a solid base of ideas about the problem area so that the connections made will push beyond the usual.

For Focused Exploration

- Set a lot of time aside to creatively explore all the approaches you want to explore.
- Make sure to work on a mix of practical and speculative approaches that matches the intensity of your original desire for a new, perhaps radically new, solution.
- Use your creativity tools liberally.

Stage 5: Initial Articulation
of a Potential Solution

By Stage 5, a lot of thinking has been done. It's time to synthesize. It's time to identify and articulate the single best emerging potential solution (or several potential solutions, if you've struck it rich).

The previous stage, focused exploration, usually produces more than one possibility. For David Rabkin, engaging museum visitors in solving a puzzle, the idea that he termed "ship on the rocks," became the most intriguing realization of his wished-for bungee jumping experience, although he felt there were other ideas that had potential as well.

Years ago a new-product group at Gillette generated a rich and broad range of wishes or approaches, selected several for focused exploration, and ultimately pursued one as a possible solution. They pursued the wish for a hair treatment that "would concentrate only on the hairs on the head that most needed help." The resulting product, Silkience, does just that.[8]

As the time comes for articulating a potential solution, use patience, boldness, and street-savvy. Given a wealth of possibilities and short-term pressure, many people feel that they must get on with it. A quick decision on one efficient solution obviates all earlier creative efforts. By contrast, other people so enjoy the creative moment and so fear implementation that they cycle continuously through the creation of more new forms of each wished-for solution and thus forestall the realization of a final solution. And a few people try to finesse making a decision by grouping all ideas into generic categories, believing that the right solution will emerge from the classification. In fact, classification sacrifices the creativity that lies in the detail of each idea and ends up yielding homogenized solutions that nobody carries through.

When the possibilities and the short-term pressures mount, resist the urges to get on with a snap decision or create infinite possibilities or homogenize. This is a moment for measured advance. Patiently and fully articulate the potential solutions developed around each selected and explored wish or approach. Take the time to understand how these potential solutions might evolve into part of the solution.

Articulating solutions, like selection, benefits from having one individual, ideally the problem owner, synthesize strains of thought in perhaps unlikely combinations. The person should be able to get away with saying, "This isn't a viably realized solution as is, but it's intriguing, and I think we can workshop it further to make it viable." At this stage, Citibank had eight robust solutions to the problem they faced, Nabisco had a couple of hundred new product possibilities, and Rabkin had six exhibit possibilities but also a favorite.

Returning to the simple ranking diagnostic he used earlier to see if he was making creative progress, Rabkin rated the "ship on the rocks" idea for "newness." He gave it a rating of 7, which was encouragingly high. Plus the idea was consistent with the museum's educational philosophy and had potential for expansion.

Now Rabkin was prompted to spend more time thoroughly articulating "ship on the rocks" to the point of understanding that a whole new class of exhibits could spring from this sort of puzzle-based engagement with the museum visitor before, during, and after a visit. While assuming a stance that "thinking on the solution is not over yet," he saw that "ship on the rocks" was clearly worth further development.

For Initial Articulation of a Potential Solution   Orient your mind toward synthesis; pull all your creative ideas together and hold onto your freshest and most exciting thoughts, even as you start thinking more practically. Don't rush it—there's still plenty of time for changing and adjusting your potential solutions.

Stage 6: Development and Transformation

The sixth stage, developing and transforming alternate potential solutions, involves a thorough and sympathetic evaluation and a fine-tuning of the potential solutions articulated in the previous stage. Only when leaving this stage will the idea finally be ready for broad-based testing (if needed), decision, and implementation.

Hold back; please don't leap ahead to that implementation now. If you do, you're likely to have to start the problem solving all over again. The best approach is to treat all prior thinking as a storehouse of emerging solutions, pull out a few potential solutions for immediate consideration, and leave others in the storehouse, ready to be developed later.

Nabisco drew ninety concepts from the two hundred possibilities for the development process. In three days of sorting, it fine-tuned them, prioritized them, and emerged with forty-five concepts to carry forward. The others were not discarded; they were reserved for development if and when needed.

By this point in his creative problem solving, Rabkin had generated twenty wishes and seven different ideas for his bungee jumping wish. He decided to focus on developing seven ideas around bungee jumping and turn to the other wished-for solutions later.

We asked him to select two ideas—one that was a favorite and one that was only mildly interesting to him—from among the seven ideas for bungee jumping and write each down on a separate sheet of paper. Rabkin's favorite was engaging museum visitors in solving the puzzle of how to save a "ship on the rocks" using the tools of science. For his other potential solution, he chose to explore videos to prepare visitors' expectations for the exhibits they would encounter.

Creativity Tool for Individuals: Forcing Positives

To raise Rabkin's level of interest and curiosity, we asked him to list the benefits of both "ship on the rocks" and the videos. With "ship on the rocks" he anticipated four solid and by now predictable benefits. With the video idea he imagined three benefits, among them a fortuitous infection as the video reached untold numbers of people over the Internet like a beneficial virus.

When we asked him if he now felt any friendlier to either form of solution, he said he felt the same about the "ship on the rocks" puzzle, but the viral spreading potential of the video, which he had not thought about before, had increased his appreciation of that idea.

Next we asked him to consider steps he would take to implement each idea and then if that practical visualization made him more receptive to either idea. The interest in the puzzle idea remained strong. The video idea, however, continued to come more alive.

We have presented this two-part exercise to hundreds of business people, and as a rule they find that about half of their ideas become more compelling as a result. There is no discernable pattern to show which step—listing the benefits or listing ways of implementation—increases the interest. Our hypothesis is that the contemplation of any idea without searching for flaws or risk brings the idea, the wished-for solution, inside your defensive barriers as a problem solver so that you can work purely on its potential. By the time he began this exercise, Rabkin may not have been prepared to risk liking another idea as much as or more than bungee jumping. After the exercise, he knew he could use the video solution.

Creativity Tool for Teams: Itemized Response

The itemized response is a tool that helps develop and transform possible solutions and raises the level of commitment from stakeholders in the group, thus easing eventual implementation.

In the first step, someone chooses the articulation of one potential solution, usually basing the choice largely on a hunch that with more creative work a final and exciting solution will emerge.

In the second step, all team members list the benefits of enacting the possible solution. When people evaluate a solution for its benefits, they not only enrich the solution but become emotionally invested in its success—an investment that will be necessary if the solution is to survive skeptical examination outside the group.

The third step in the itemized response is to search for flaws in the possible solution. Most people move to this step first, hoping to save time by weeding out obviously bad ideas quickly. But then you end up being so rough on new ideas that you lose them all. Instead, look for the benefits first. After that, search for flaws forgivingly; view the flaws as difficulties to be straightened out rather than as reasons to stop considering the potential solution altogether. It helps to frame flaws productively by articulating them as "how" questions. For instance, instead of saying "That will cost too much," which causes people to stop right there, say, "How do we get the money for it?" which invites further constructive thought.

The fourth step is to straighten out the concerns uncovered during the search for flaws. Tackle the gravest concern first, because if that can't be overcome, there's no need to spend time on the others. This step requires as much creativity and self-control as all the previous steps combined.

A food manufacturer's group was in the middle of giving an itemized response to a fresh, refrigerated product to add to its traditional "boxed" line. The product was promising but tricky in terms of the company's traditional distribution. Instead of simply throwing the idea away with a quick "That won't fit," the product development group asked, "How do we distribute it?" The group worked hard and creatively, and eventually they thought up a unique delivery procedure that they could use as a market experiment and that wouldn't require them to change the way they worked with the current distributors. The group became so enthusiastic about the new delivery procedure that they went on to create several new refrigerated versions of other products.

The fifth step is to sum up the potential solution in the context of its benefits and its flaws and the modifications necessary to overcome the flaws. Nabisco emerged from focused exploration, articulation, and the first stages of development and transformation with a prioritized list of forty-five concepts or potential solutions, a testing methodology, and a decision to take the top twelve concepts to the first round of testing. Citibank prioritized from forty concepts to eight, decided that they were all so different and the problem so complicated that, as Jackie Burton said, "We'll probably try them all." David Rabkin summed up by saying, "The first video will tempt people to see and prepare them to experience a major new exhibit in the museum. We will produce it in collaboration with an industry partner involved in Web site construction and an author and artist interested in working with us. The names of the industry partner and the artist will appear in the credits and as well as in the museum's press. The partner will donate some of the work, and the artists will be paid."

The sixth and final step of itemized response is to lay out the actions necessary to go forward into implementation with the potential solution. At Citibank, Jackie Burton took over full coordination of readying the potential solutions and monitoring how Y2K was going to play out. Nabisco laid out a research plan with dates, tasks, and responsibilities. Rabkin listed the beginning steps needed to gain museum approval and noted ideas for enlisting the participation of others.

For Development and Transformation

- Recognize that this stage is generally different for individuals and groups.
- Adjust your potential solutions until they better fit your goal and the problem you're addressing.
- Enumerate the benefits of your potential solutions to offset the natural instinct to weed out the new.
- Look at the flaws as difficulties to work out so that the solutions can work.
- Adjust your solutions to the demands of your problem until everyone in the creative team unites behind the solution.
- List enough steps to get moving toward implementation.

Stage 7: Implementation

Implementing a solution often requires more creative effort than getting to the solution. This is true for focused exploration and for overcoming flaws, it is true again for implementation. The need to stay creative grows at every stage. Difficult as it is to generate radically imaginative wishes, it is often more difficult to transform the wishes into practical solutions. Taking a solution into a world that has not helped create the solution, a world naturally resistant to the new, presents even more challenges. We address implementation in a few pages here, but it is in fact a subject that could fill its own book.

Perhaps most important is to frame implementation not as an end but as a continuation of creative endeavor over the long term. By the publication date of this book, Nabisco will have launched three products from the work outlined in this chapter; nine more products will be approaching launch, and another thirty-three will still be under consideration. And certainly other product development groups will be moving through groundwork and immersion in the quest for the next generation of products.

The solution that finds its way through implementation into the many parts of a company and eventually into the outside world necessarily has many owners, only a few of whom have been directly involved in creating the original solution. The rest are won over. By carefully involving the critical people in implementation, the original problem solvers can build a coalition in which everyone feels he or she is part of the solution. As this coalition grows, everyone's sense of ownership and support adds to the probability of successful implementation. Problem solvers, whether groups or individuals, who consider carefully whom to involve from the very beginning of the process of groundwork and immersion, find it easier to get a solution accepted throughout an organization, and this makes implementation more likely.

Turning colleagues into advocates requires understanding the various forms resistance to new ideas takes, which in turn requires understanding each phase of implementation. The solution needs to be broken into tasks. A new product, for example, needs a marketing strategy, including positioning, naming, packaging, brand development, and promotion. It also needs an implementation strategy, including manufacturing, channel development and distribution, financial planning and budgeting, resources, speed, and so on. Each of these discrete areas can be handled creatively using strategies and tools similar to those that were involved in creating the solution.

Identify the owners and contributors on each tricky part of the solution, and use a facilitator in meetings throughout the implementation process to help establish a nonthreatening, productive coalition for implementation. Try to engage the intrinsic motivation of an implementation coalition's increasing membership to keep creativity alive and avoid letting fear or resentment undermine commitment to change. Keep the process flexible and communication flowing to help people adapt new information and adjust the solution to fit the environment.

Once a solution is implemented, applaud the creative work of the problem solvers and the implementing coalition. Appreciation will enhance those people's readiness to address the next opportunity or problem in a creative way.

To ensure that a product is ready when it emerges for broad evaluation and to be sure that its reception in the company at large is not altogether arbitrary, Nabisco uses a traditional "stage-gate" process in their new product development. As Wayne Puglia explains, "We have three guiding questions, 'Can we make it?' 'Can we sell it?' and 'Can we make money at it?' Our stage-gate process is designed to answer these questions" as products advance in development to inexpensive trials and then sequentially more costly trials. The first stage involves assessing consumer need, concept development, and a BASES test for initial consumer appeal. If a product concept survives these assessments, it goes through the gate to Stage 2, where prototypes are made, technical and financial feasibility is assessed, consumers refine the concepts through qualitative testing, and a simulated test market helps determine the size of market and sale and repeat purchase volumes. The concepts that survive these tests go on to Stage 3, where they are manufactured on a limited basis and receive preliminary advertising and financial projections. Consumer purchase rates are scrutinized, and there's often a full-blown consumer test in "thirty cities or so," although, as Puglia notes, "the speed at which competition moves now makes these market tests dangerous. Sometimes they can copy our products in the open-to-the-public testing phase and get them to market at the same time we do." If this stage ends successfully, it's followed by a detailed proposal to the company for funding the new product or business. The performance required of the product that advances through the three stages of refinement makes funding and acceptance of the product easy to justify, even for complete newcomers to the product and its development.

David Rabkin proceeded with his "ship on the rocks" puzzle in part by enlisting support for the idea generation process. He and a few colleagues ran a workshop over several days to orient twenty-five staff members to the latest thinking about educational goals and about particular ideas under consideration, including "ship on the rocks." Then the staff worked on generating new ideas themselves, thereby shaping and taking ownership of the future museum experience. If Rabkin had hurried to create his "ship on the rocks" puzzle experience and had kept his colleagues' focus on that one effort, he might not have won universal enthusiasm for the exhibit. What's more, the one exhibit might have been all the museum gained from his work. Instead, because he invited colleagues to get involved in the play of the whole problem-solving effort, people got behind the original idea of the puzzle and collectively fleshed it out into a whole new archetype for the museum experience. Rabkin had exactly what he wanted— an archetype that can be used again and again over time in any number of exhibits. Visitors to the museum can now encounter a variety of real-world puzzles to arouse their curiosity and subsequently put related science and technology to work extricating the "ship on the rocks" or doing whatever the puzzle may require.

Jackie Burton at Citibank kept potential solutions ready for quick implementation right up to the last minute of the Y2K changeover. In effect, Citibank was prepared with solutions for whatever problem might occur.

For Implementation   Enlist the world outside your creative team into a coalition supporting your solutions.

Structures That Support Purposeful Creativity

Some companies have formal strategies to enrich evolving solutions and keep them open to further creative input throughout development. Nabisco, like many organizations, uses a stage-gate process in which new product concepts pause in their development at certain predetermined milestones for review of work to date and formal approval to go to the next stage.[9] Besides controlling risk, the stage-gate pauses allow fresh creative perspective to strengthen the potential product; both aspects of the process reinforce commitment to the product.

John Wallingford of Wyeth Nutritional has institutionalized another structure to keep purposeful creativity and innovation flowing. Wyeth solicits new product or process ideas from within the company annually, and every year a fresh team considers all submissions, improving and adjusting them to the purposes of the business. Then the team selects the most appropriate ideas for funding in the current year. Submissions that don't fit one year's strategy are returned to the author, with the reviewers' comments, for modification and are automatically included in the next year's round for consideration. If an idea fails to make the cut two years running, it is not included automatically for consideration a third year, but it may be resubmitted by its creator.[10]

Just as it makes good sense to support creative problem solving, it makes good sense to avoid permanently killing off solutions that don't reach the stage of implementation. The world changes and needs change, so innovations are needed continually. Ideas that don't work today could be critical to the solution of a problem tomorrow. Many organizations find ways to capture and store ideas, subsequently pursuing them when the time is right. Creative organizations infuse creative capacity into long-term research initiatives that produce new thinking year after year. For example, the space program in the United States has identified 1,400 spin-offs from its work; thousands of products have resulted from ongoing research in university and government laboratories; Bell Labs was responsible for over 26,000 patents and eleven Nobel Prizes.[11]

While there is a burgeoning and valuable science around short-term creativity and innovation with initiatives called "fast failure" and "success transfer," in the long run short-term innovation alone will leave a company at a loss when the first competitor radically changes the game. Establishing permanent systemic creativity and instituting formal measures that encourage and capture rich and speculative thought from every creative problem-solving effort will boost a company's innovation potential well into the future. The need for formal, longer-term, less-focused creative work as part of an organization's strategy grows as competition grows and business environments evolve. Microsoft invested $5 billion in long-term research in 2001 alone to be sure it stayed on top for the long term.[12]

And just as companies will do well to look beyond purely short-term creativity and innovation, so too they will benefit by structuring the purview of their creative problem solving to range beyond development of new product. Companies can profitably apply purposeful creativity techniques to planning, policy, human resources, finance, manufacturing, information technology, communications, administration, marketing, distribution, and sales. When a company is creative in all its parts, it can bring purposeful creative thinking to bear wherever and however the need for an innovative solution arises.

EIGHT

Sustaining
the Change

As THE CHANGE to systemic creativity goes forward, everything covered in the introduction and the first seven chapters—from the dynamics of the creative process and their relationship to individuals and companies, through personal and corporate climate, through leadership and innovation—requires continued attention, reinforcement, exercise, follow-through, and reinvention. Creativity doesn't have to stop, and you don't want it to stop. Yet the forces against it are so strong that, without continued reinforcement and reinvention, it will fall away. Plan on sustaining creativity systemically into the indefinite future. Record the returns it produces. Be ready for the hiccups of resistance it will encounter—there will be many—and carry on with a cheerleader's enthusiasm and with the knowledge that creativity works and makes a vital difference.

Plan Ahead

Every company has different variables for how it plans around the particulars of its own climate and delivers the elements of support necessary to its own creative projects in whatever stage of process. The important thing is to keep the plan going and keep the planning flexible. As Terry Egger, publisher of the St. Louis *Post-Dispatch,* says, "You have to have a plan in place, but not one so rigid that you don't take detours. All the 'Aha's' are in the detours."[1]

As circumstances evolve and as employees come up with new ideas, any plan for sustaining creative change will itself change, and change creatively. Eric Steidinger, a director at Jack Morton Worldwide, says, "We have a thousand brilliant people spread out in thirty markets around the world, each trying to achieve the same vision, and sometimes they come up with things that weren't part of the original plan. We have to recognize what they find that is different and good and incorporate that on purpose into what we do."[2]

At the point systemic creativity really gets traction and becomes embedded throughout a company, evidence of the change—creative activity, the actual creative changes—will come fast and furious and all over the company. This is a good thing. It's what you want. But centralized planning can get overloaded.

In large environments of rapid and widespread change, effective creative planning is largely decentralized planning that's tolerant of risk and ambiguity.[3] The United States is an interesting example of decentralized planning. This is a large organization of tremendous complexity in which innovation thrives over the long term. Governance is kept as close to the customer as possible. Frequent investments by the central authority are designed and executed locally. Elegant checks and balances permit radical experiments to be started and to be tempered only later and if necessary for the common good. There is a deep respect for the individual, and there is an expectation that while a massive amount of creativity and innovation will occur under the large umbrella of protection provided by the central authority, it will not by and large be the central authority that comes up with the creative ideas.

This analogy isn't intended to stretch to "one person, one vote." We would suggest, however, that much is gained through a broad participation in shaping corporate strategy as well as creative strategy by both creative executives and employees with experience doing creative work close to the customer. And always creativity moves the company forward most effectively when it's practiced by people at all levels who understand and commit to the values and the vision of the company and its leadership. Whether centralized or decentralized, planning for ongoing creativity is itself an ongoing act of creativity.

Record Results

Keep track of the results creativity produces. But at least initially, keep track of them in a manner somewhat separate from short-term corporate profitability projections. Not only does an organic corporate change to systemic creativity take time, the results of the change take time to surface. And pressure to show profitability too quickly can stop the change to creativity dead. As Citibank's Sam Borenstein says, "Innovation takes three to five years to prove itself. You need to give yourself at least that much time or you will ultimately fail."

To begin with, monitor evidence that signals the growing root strength of creativity in the organization. Statistical data will be elusive, but you can survey employees for perception of safety, fear of failure, autonomy, interest in and satisfaction from work, access to diverse information, challenge, frequency and effectiveness of new ideas, support, barriers, teams, and coalitions. These indicators may seem painfully distant from the bottom line, but they describe the health and spread of creativity in a company, and they have everything to do with creative solutions.

William Hamlin, president, North America, of container shipping line APL/NOL, says, "I face continual pressure to deliver conventional measures. Yet I need to encourage the field to balance their traditional budget with their new creative mode. I've told the field not to worry so much about reports to headquarters yet. I'll worry about those."[4]

The longer and more deeply creativity sets into a company, the more the value can be seen in the environment and production and appear on the bottom line. Well into its creativity change program, APL/NOL may not yet have established a direct relationship between creative work and weekly reporting, but creative changes have nonetheless brought financial improvement that's measurable to some degree. Hamlin says, "We have seen both immediate and long-term results, especially in areas of cost reduction and avoidance, revenues, and asset management. Eleven periods into the program we have measured an impact of $46.6 million." Hamlin believes that over time a creativity metric will emerge that is at once creative, true, and able to give an encompassing picture of profitability.

Sam Borenstein at Citibank is working on that:

Our current key metric today is captured in a simple formula: Divide the revenue we get from innovation by total revenue. But revenues are a lagging indicator. Beneath this metric we are measuring many different things, such as what's in the pipeline, the number of ideas generated and the number of ideas implemented, cycle time for product development, incremental versus nonincremental revenue. We also look at . . . new product, success transfer, new business models, and channel innovations. In our analyses we are trying to develop stochastic models, new types of statistical projection techniques that will give us a better handle for planning and measuring innovation.

Regardless of your own success at monitoring definable results, understand that, given the chance and time, creativity can infuse almost every employee and enhance almost every performance. And the value of creativity radiates into virtually all results of any kind.

Aware of the absolute fundamental value that creative people bring to a company, Mark Greiner at Steelcase believes, "When we don't allow everyone to be creative, we cannot arrive at the best potential solution."[5] Steve Leichtman at Tufts Health Care Plan talks about the transcendent worth of "spreading creativity to every pocket of the company." Kathy Lundberg of Guidant says, "We cannot tell everyone they are supposed to be creative; that's too much pressure. But we can and must afford everyone the opportunity and build wide appreciation for creative thought." There are other and measurable results, but none is more important than a company full of creative people.

Expect Resistance

Count on resistance to change in general and to creativity in particular. It's part of the human condition, often for good reason, and it will live on not just as companies change toward creativity but as creativity itself generates change. To keep creativity manifest for the long haul, you have to make sure it transforms, outlasts, or overrides the resistance—or that it uses resistance productively.

Remember that resistance can be a virtue. It can occur because others see something for which the creative solution has not accounted. Bill Wilson, formerly vice president of innovation at Kimberly-Clark, was a wise mentor to a number of people who aspired to be leaders of innovation. Frequently his protégés would be frustrated by resistance to new ideas they were promoting. Part of his advice was to welcome the resistance. His position was that if you are open-minded and if even part of the resistance is an accurate assessment of problems, you are better off—now you can make a better solution with a higher probability of success. Even if the resistance is not based on a sound business assessment and is more emotional self-protection, it is still useful information since it gives you an understanding of how others feel and what you might do to deal with it preemptively. Wilson's shorthand to convey this was "Facts are your friends."[6] Better than most people, Wilson knew that resistance was an inevitable part of the creative process—something to expect, even to welcome, and then to address.

In the spirit of Wilson's practical acceptance of resistance, we offer this quote from Upton Sinclair: "It is difficult to get a man to understand something when his salary depends upon his not understanding it."[7] This statement captures clearly an important issue. Innovation, a change in the order of things, may be a threat to some people's positions. Those people's resistance is neither unnatural nor immaterial. Resistance to creativity is a surfacing of issues that need to be addressed. Broadly speaking, resistance is one more call, one more arena, for continuous creativity.

Much emotional resistance to the simple fact of change succumbs to training and the subsequent firsthand experience of what one's own creative potential can accomplish. Involving employees in setting goals also productively channels the energy that might otherwise go into defending the status quo. Independent people who choose common goals for themselves don't just get behind the goals; they get behind them creatively because they already have a leg up on their creative motivation.

You can simply expect the resistance and recruit potentially disaffected groups for early participation in and ownership of creativity changes. You can also remain open to the resistance and learn from it. "Sometimes I get frustrated because I want this to happen faster, but I'm face to face with the reality of what it takes to achieve widespread organizational change and growth," says Eric Steidinger of Jack Morton Worldwide. "I know I can't be dogmatic as a leader. I have to stay focused on driving the pride and be open to the idea that people who aren't evolving in the direction I want might have good reasons not to, or they may be doing something that I'm missing."

As soon as you overcome resistance in one arena, it will show itself in another. Don't be surprised. Don't despair. With a little help, creativity will not just survive but prevail.

You may be surprised sometimes to encounter not resistance but exhaustion. The change to creativity involves stress and hard work. Creative problem solving itself involves hard work, especially while it's still new work. People get tired, so cheer them up. Celebrate short-term successes. Remind people that not only does creativity work, it matters.

To keep its creative momentum going, the St. Louis *Post-Dispatch* developed a sort of therapeutic narrative. Publisher Terry Egger involved the whole company in constructing a story "with heroes and villains and a plot" about the newspaper itself on a quest to win back an audience wooed away by television and the Internet. The story drew employees into their own narrative-centered coalition committed to bringing the *Post-Dispatch* back to glory. As the change to creativity went on, the paper overcame obstacles one by one, and, says Egger, "As we fixed each point, everyone could see the immediate upside impact." But Egger acknowledges:

> *There will always be grievances and disappointments. Certain changes mean that people have to put up with seemingly intolerable circumstances for a period of time. There are also times when the future gets lost in the boring daily grind of execution. Each time we find ourselves losing momentum or questioning the relevance of what we're doing, we resurrect the story and recount where we are in it.*

Every celebration of creative success reinvigorates commitment to creativity. When the celebration ties the success to a potent common vision of a company's future, renewed vigor and commitment acquire deeper and more lasting purchase.

Encourage the Flow of Information

When knowledge about available technologies reaches marketing people who have been keyed into customer needs by direct contact as well as by salespeople, and when their combined information flows to corporate planners in touch with investment and financing possibilities, then purposeful creativity can deliver solutions on a range of fronts. Information makes a difference in any company. In a creative company, it becomes essential daily fuel. Lacking information, creativity dries up. Lacking proper information, creativity loses effectiveness.

Information is the fluid expression of knowledge feeding the creative effort. Keep it available, keep it rich and diverse, keep it flowing. And remember to keep it flowing up to leadership, not just horizontally or from the top down. People in power often don't get all the unpleasant news. Subordinates won't pass it up for a host of reasons, sometimes because superiors don't want to hear it, sometimes because it reveals subordinate ineptitude. In either case, stonewalling prevents leadership from providing balanced guidance. And many creative people, particularly in middle management, are reluctant to pass on ideas to someone higher in the organization when the ideas still hold risks and flaws. As a result, leaders don't learn about many of the creative ideas lower in the organization. We encourage leaders to maintain the greatest possible contact throughout the company to augment the good but synthesized information they get from direct reports. Similarly, we encourage leaders to stay in touch with customers—customer dissatisfaction can be a great springboard for new ideas, and customer dissatisfaction seldom reaches leaders in raw form.

We've discussed several companies as examples of successful creativity. None of the leaders of those companies feel that they have creativity fully in hand. None feel that their companies have achieved complete and lasting systemic creativity. Most would be hesitant to predict that they could ever fully achieve it. All remain intent on achieving it and continue to pursue it vigorously—and creatively.

If you have read this book at the start of or in the midst of a corporate change to creativity, we hope you have found useful information, and we wish you and your organization well. We also urge you to remember that the work of successful creativity continues. If you and your organization have the resolve to carry on, the creative effort you undertake now will continue. In evolving forms, the effort will begin again and still continue. The rewards that creativity brings will continue and renew as well.

PREFACE

1. W. J. J. Gordon, "An Operational Approach to Creativity," *Harvard Business Review* 36, no. 6 (November–December 1956).

2. George M. Prince, *The Practice of Creativity* (New York: Harper & Row, 1970).

INTRODUCTION

1. The Steelcase story is told in parts throughout this book. The story was constructed through a series of interviews with Lee Bloomquist, Fred Faiks, Mark Greiner, Peter Jeff, Jim Keene, Dave Lathrop, Rick Mohr, Sue Sacks, and Jack Tanis over the winter and spring of 2000.

2. George Whalin, quoted in "Montgomery Ward Closes Shop," Associated Press; December 28, 2000. The Bogs' Historical Clothing Web site contains the history of Montgomery Ward. See <http://histclo.hispeed.com/fashion/store/mail/his/mcat-his/>.

3. Rosabeth M. Kanter, *When Giants Learn to Dance: Mastering the Challenges of Strategy, Management, and Careers in the 1990s* (New York: Simon & Schuster, 1989), 19–20.

4. Richard A. D'Aveni and Robert Gunther, *Hypercompetition: Managing the Dynamics of Strategic Maneuvering* (New York: Free Press, 1994), 8.

5. Teresa M. Amabile, *Creativity in Context* (Boulder, CO: Westview Press, 1996), 250–253, 35. "A product or response will be judged as creative to the extent that (a) it is both a novel and appropriate, useful, correct

or valuable response to the task at hand, and (b) the task is heuristic rather than algorithmic. . . . This conceptual definition is closely aligned with [that of many other theorists], in its inclusion of novelty and appropriateness as two hallmarks of creativity."

6. *Webster's New Universal Unabridged Dictionary,* ed. Jean L. Mc-Kechnie (New York: Dorset & Baber, 1983), 945. "Innovation: the act of innovating or effecting a change in the established order; introduction of something new."

CHAPTER 1

1. George Land and Beth Jarman, *Breakpoint and Beyond: Mastering the Future Today* (New York: Harper Business, 1992), 1533–1534; Teresa M. Amabile, *Growing Up Creative* (Buffalo, NY: Creative Education Foundation Press, 1985), chapter 3; Teresa M. Amabile, *Creativity in Context* (Boulder, CO: Westview Press, 1996), 250–253, 260–261.

2. Jordan B. Peterson, *Maps of Meaning: The Architecture of Belief* (New York: Routledge, 1999), 22–30.

3. Perls, Frederick S., *Gestalt Therapy Verbatim* (New York: Bantam Books, 1974), as quoted in Mary E. Scott, "How Stress Can Affect Gifted/Creative Potential: Ideas to Better Insure Realization of Potential," *Creative Child and Adult Quarterly* 10, no. 4 (Winter 1985): 240–249. Also see Frederick S. Perls, *In and Out of the Garbage Pail* (Lafayette, CA: Real People Press, 1969). "After closure this gestalt (response of an organism to a situation, which is taken as an unanalyzable and indivisible whole) will recede into the background, to empty the foreground for another emergent or emergency. . . . It will not disappear, be forgotten or repressed. It will remain in the aliveness of the figure/background exchange."

4. Heiko Lotz, interview by Jeff Mauzy, tape recording, New York, 8 September 1999. All subsequent Lotz quotes are from this interview.

5. Abraham H. Maslow, *Motivation and Personality* (New York: Harper and Row, 1954), 210, 214–215. According to Maslow, some of the characteristics of people as they grow toward the highest stage of self-actualization are "their ease of penetration to reality, their closer approach to an animal-like or child-like acceptance and spontaneity, [which] imply a superior awareness of their own impulses, their own desires, opinions, and subjective reactions in general. . . . Self-actualized people have a wonderful capacity to appreciate again and again, freshly and naively, the basic goods of life with awe, pleasure, wonder, and even ecstasy, however stale these experiences may be for other people."

6. Teresa M. Amabile, "Motivation and Creativity: Effects of Motivational Orientation on Creative Writers," *Journal of Personality and Social Psychology* 48 (1985): 393–399; Amabile, *Creativity in Context,* 107–110.

7. Amabile, *Creativity in Context,* 115–119.

8. Kurt Miller, interview by Jeff Mauzy, tape recording, Boston, MA, 22 April 1999. All subsequent Miller quotes are from this interview.

9. Peterson, *Maps of Meaning,* 43. "The most rapidly activated of these two systems governs inhibition or ongoing behavior, cessation of currently goal-directed activity. The second, equally powerful but somewhat more conservative, underlies exploration, general behavior activation, and forward locomotion. Operation of the former appears associated with anxiety, with fear and apprehension, with negative affect—universal subjective responses to the threatening and unexpected. Operation of the latter, by contrast, appears associated with hope, with curiosity and interest, with positive affect—subjective responses to the promising and unexpected. The process of exploring the emergent unknown is therefore guided by the interplay between the emotions of curiosity/hope/excitement on the one hand and anxiety on the other—or to describe the phenomenon from another viewpoint, between the different motor systems responsible for approach (forward locomotion) and inhibition of ongoing behavior."

10. Peterson, *Maps of Meaning,* 19–20.

11. Mary Ann Robatt, interview by Jeff Mauzy, tape recording, Boston, MA, 8 March 1999. All subsequent Robatt quotes are from this interview.

12. Jeffrey A. Gray and Neil McNaughton, "The Neuropsychology of Anxiety: Reprise," in Debra A. Hope et al., eds., "Perspectives on Anxiety, Panic, and Fear," *Current Theory and Research in Motivation* 43 (1996): 6–134. See also Steven E. Hyman, "Briefing on the Brain-Body Connection" (paper presented to the U.S. House of Representatives, Subcommittee on Labor, DHHS, Education and Related Agencies, Washington, D.C., 5 November, 977); Thomas B. Czerner, *What Makes You Tick: The Brain in Plain English* (New York: John Wiley, 2001), 40.

13. Amabile, *Creativity in Context,* 234–235. Amabile's work tested a company during downsizing. It found that the anticipation of downsizing had a most deleterious impact, with creativity remaining depressed long after productivity returned to normal. See also Teresa M. Amabile and R. Conti, "Changes in the Work Environment for Creativity During Downsizing," *Academy of Management Journal* 42, no. 6 (1999): 630–640.

14. Jordan B. Peterson, unrecorded conversation with Jeff Mauzy, Cambridge, MA, August 1999.

15. P. A. Okebukola, "Relationships Among Anxiety Belief Systems and Creativity," *Journal of Social Psychology* 126, no. 6 (1986): 815–816; Kinnard White, "Anxiety, Extroversion-Introversion, and Divergent Thinking Ability," *Journal of Creative Behavior* 2, no. 2 (1968): 199–127; Gerald Matthews, "The Effects of Anxiety on Intellectual Performance," *Journal of Research in Personality* 20 (1986): 385–401; Arieh Y. Shalev, "Stress vs. Traumatic Stress: From Acute Homeostatic Reactions to Chronic Psychopathology," in *Traumatic Stress: The Effects of Overwhelming Experience on Mind, Body, and Society,* ed. Bessel A. van der Kolk, Alexander C. McFarland, and Lars Weisaeth (New York: Guilford Press, 1996), 77–101.

16. Peterson, *Maps of Meaning,* 19–20. "The brain has one mode of operation when in explored territory and another when in unexplored territory. In the unexplored world, caution—expressed in fear and behavioral immobility—initially predominates, but may be superseded by curiosity—expressed in hope, excitement and, above all, creative exploratory behavior. Creative exploration of the unknown, and consequent generation of knowledge, is construction or update of patterns of behavior and representation, such that the unknown is transformed from something terrifying and compelling into something beneficial (or at least something irrelevant)."

17. Peter McGhee, interview by Jeff Mauzy, tape recording,Boston, MA, 3 April 2000. All subsequent McGhee quotes are from this interview.

18. See <http://www.discoverfrance.net/France/Art/Picasso/Picasso.shtml>.

19. Czerner, *What Makes You Tick,* chapters 7 and 8; John S. Dacey and Kathleen H. Lennon, *Understanding Creativity: The Interplay of Biological, Psychological, and Social Factors* (San Francisco: Jossey-Bass, 1998), 153–171, 189–201; J. W. Getzels and M. Csikszentmihalyi, "From Problem-Solving to Problem-Finding," in *Perspectives in Creativity,* ed. I. A. Taylor and J. W. Getzels (Chicago: Aldine, 1975), 9–116; Stephen M. Kosslyn and Olivier Koenig, *Wet Mind: The New Cognitive Neuroscience* (New York: Free Press, 1995), 52–107, 128–215, 341–361, 387–400; Jordi E. Obiols, "Art and Creativity: Neuropsychological Perspectives," in *Depression and the Spiritual in Modern Art: Homage to Mind,* ed. J. J. Schildkraut (New York: John Wiley & Sons, 1994), 33–47; Daniel Reisberg, *Cognition: Exploring the Science of the Mind* (New York: W. W. Norton, 1997), 124–157, 257–303.

20. Jeff Mauzy, "Managing Personal Creativity," in *Innovationsforschung und Technologie Management* (Berlin and Heidelberg: Springer-Verlag, 1999), 27.

21. Ibid., 26.

22. Min Basadur, "Optimal Ideation-Evaluation Ratios," *Creativity Research Journal* 8, no. 1 (1995): 63–75.

CHAPTER 2

1. Sun Tzu, *The Art of War,* ed. James Clavell (London: Hodder and Stoughton, 1981), 26.

2. Jordan B. Peterson, *Maps of Meaning: The Architecture of Belief* (New York: Routledge, 1999), 75–76. "As parents are to children, cultures are to adults: we do not know how the patterns we act out (or the concepts we utilize) originated, or what precise 'purposes' (what long-term 'goals') they currently serve. . . . Furthermore, we cannot describe such patterns well, abstractly (explicitly, semantically), even though we duplicate them accurately (and unconsciously) in our behavior." But the story can have a happy ending. Peterson goes forward: "The fact of our sociability ensures that our adaptive behaviors are structured with the social community in mind, at least in the long run, and increases our chances of exposure to creative intelligence. . . . In this manner, we obtain the skills of others. Our capacity for abstraction allows us to take our facility for imitation one step further, however: we can learn to imitate not only the precise behaviors that constitute adaptation, but the process by which those behaviors were generated. This means we can learn not only skill, but meta-skill (can learn to mimic the pattern of behavior that generates new skills). It is the encapsulation of meta-skill in a story that makes that story great."

3. Carl. R. Rogers, *On Becoming a Person: A Therapist's View of Psychotherapy* (Boston and New York: Houghton Mifflin, 1961), 169. "Many of the serious criticisms of our culture and its trends may best be formulated in terms of a dearth of creativity. Let us state some of these very briefly: In education we tend to turn to conformists, stereotypes, individuals whose education is 'completed,' rather than freely creative and original thinkers . . . . In industry, creation is reserved for the few—the manager, the designer, the head of the research department—while for the many life is devoid of original or creative endeavor. . . . To be original, or different, is felt to be 'dangerous.' Why be concerned over this? If, as a people, we enjoy conformity rather than creativity, shall we not be permitted this choice? In my estimation such a choice would be entirely reasonable were it not for one great shadow which hangs over all of us. In a time when knowledge, constructive and destructive, is advancing by the most incredible leaps and bounds into a fantastic atomic age, genuinely creative adaptation seems to represent the only possibility that man can keep abreast of the kaleidoscopic change in his world." (p. 348)

4. Robert Fritz, *The Path of Least Resistance: Learning to Become the Creative Force in Your Own Life,* Expanded Edition (New York: Fawcett Books, 1989), chapters 6, 8, 9.

5. Teresa Amabile, unrecorded conversation with Jeff Mauzy, Boston, MA, May 2000.

6. Annie Gaudreault, interview by Jeff Mauzy, tape recording, Toronto, 10 February 1999. All subsequent Gaudreault quotes are from this interview.

7. Edmund J. Bourne, *The Anxiety and Phobia Workbook,* 3rd ed. (Oakland, CA: New Harbinger Publications, 2000), 200–203.

8. John Gibson, interview by Jeff Mauzy, tape recording, Houston, TX, 26 February 2000. All subsequent Gibson quotes are from this interview.

9. Doug Farmer, unrecorded observation by Jeff Mauzy, Baton Rouge, LA, Fall 1994.

10. William Shakespeare, *Hamlet,* v. 166.

11. Paul Dietrich, interview by Jeff Mauzy and recorded in "Creativity in Corporations: A Factor Study of Highly Creative Architecture and Advertising Firms," Master's thesis, Boston University School of Business, 1985.

12. Laura Wills, interview by Jeff Mauzy, tape recording, Toronto, 10 February 1999. All subsequent Wills quotes are from this interview.

13. David Perkins, unrecorded observation by Jeff Mauzy, Cambridge, MA, 25 October 1999.

CHAPTER 3

1. Jack Tanis, interview by Jeff Mauzy, tape recording, Grand Rapids, MI, 6 February, 1999. All subsequent Tanis quotes are from this interview.

2. Jim Keene, interview by Jeff Mauzy, tape recording, Grand Rapids, MI, 6 February 1999. All subsequent Keene quotes are from this interview.

3. Jerry Hirshberg, *The Creative Priority: Driving Innovative Business in the Real World* (New York: Harper Business, 1998), 33–34; Marlene M. Turner and Anthony R. Pratkanis, "Mitigating Groupthink by Stimulating Constructive Conflict," in *Having Conflict in Organizations,* ed. Carsten K. W. De Dreu, et al. (London: Sage Publications, 1997), 53–71.

4. C. J. Nemeth, "Dissent as Driving Cognition, Attitudes, and Judgements," *Social Cognition* 13, no. 3 (Fall 1995): 273–291.

5. George Prince, lecture, Synectics, 18 December 1987.

6. Conrad Paulus, unrecorded interview by Jeff Mauzy, Armonk, NY, 27 January 1997. All subsequent Paulus quotes are from this interview.

7. Maureen Arkle, interview by Jeff Mauzy, tape recording, Waltham, MA, 3 April 1999. All subsequent Arkle quotes are from this interview.

8. Mary McKenney, interview by Jeff Mauzy, tape recording, New York, NY, 9 September 1999. All subsequent McKenney quotes are from this interview.

9. Jorge Bermudez, interview by Jeff Mauzy, tape recording, White Plains, NY, 17 November 2001. All subsequent Bermudez quotes are from this interview.

10. Sam Borenstein, interview by Jeff Mauzy, tape recording, White Plains, NY, 17 November 2001. All subsequent Borenstein quotes are from this interview.

11. Phil Hettema, interview by Jeff Mauzy, tape recording, Universal City, CA, 3 May 1999. All subsequent Hettema quotes are from this interview.

12. Howard Gardner, *Intelligence Reframed: Multiple Intelligences for the 21st Century* (New York: Basic Books, 1999), especially Chapter 3.

13. Roger Schank, *Coloring Outside the Lines: Raising a Smarter Kid by Breaking All the Rules* (New York: HarperCollins, 2000), 24.

14. "Can Imagination Be Taught?" *Supervision* 52 (November 1991): 5.

15. B. Voss, "What's the Big Idea?" *Sales and Marketing Management* 143 (July 1991): 36–41.

16. Lucien Frohling, recalled from unrecorded conversation by Jeff Mauzy, New York, NY, Winter 1994.

17. Pat Wnck, recalled from unrecorded conversation by Jeff Mauzy, Appleton, WI, Spring 1995.

18. Stephen Leichtman, interview by Jeff Mauzy, tape recording, Waltham, MA, 3 April 1999. All subsequent Leichtman quotes are from this interview.

19. Mary Sonnack, telephone interview by Jeff Mauzy, tape recording, 15 January 1999. All subsequent Sonnack quotes are from this interview.

20. "Dr. Land's Latest Bit of Magic," *Life Magazine*, 27 October 1972, 42–48.

21. Valéry-Anne Giscard d'Estaing, *The World Almanac Book of Inventions* (New York: World Almanac Publications, 1985), 159.

22. Gunter Henn, unrecorded conversation with Jeff Mauzy, Cambridge, MA, Winter 1996. Details were published by Henn Architecture, *Architekten Ingenieure,* Munich, 1998. See <http://www.info@henn.com>.

23. Philip M. Rosenzweig, "Bill Gates and the Management of Microsoft," Case 9-392-019 (Boston: Harvard Business School, 1991).

24. Editors of *Wired,* "Rocking with Mr. Bill," *Wired,* December 1994, <http://www.wired.com/wired/archive/2.12/gates.html/>; James Wallace, *Overdrive: Bill Gates and the Race to Control Cyberspace* (New York: John Wiley & Sons, 1997), 25–26; Joyce Wycoff, quote from *USA Weekend* interview with Bill Gates; see <http://www.thinksmart.com>.

25. Peter Carlin, documented notes recalled from strategy work attended by Jeff Mauzy, Summit, NJ, Fall 1994. All subsequent Carlin references come from this work.

26. Marty Finegan, documented notes recalled from strategy work attended by Jeff Mauzy, Montvale, NJ, 5 June 2000.

27. Desiree de Myer, "Envision It: What's the Big Idea?" *Smart Business Magazine,* 1 October 2001, 64–65.

28. Michael A. Cusumano and Richard W. Selby, *Microsoft Secrets: How the World's Most Powerful Company Creates Technology, Shapes Markets, and Manages People* (New York: Touchstone Press, a division of Simon & Schuster, 1995), 329–333.

29. Rosabeth M. Kanter, *The Change Masters: Innovation and Entrepreneurship in the American Corporation* (New York: Simon & Schuster, 1983), 55.

30. Ibid., 146–149.

CHAPTER 4

1. *Webster's New Universal Unabridged Dictionary,* ed. Jean L. McKechnie (New York: Dorset & Baber, 1983, 339; 444. To distinguish as cleanly as we can between the concepts climate and culture, we use the following portion of the definition of "climate": "any prevailing conditions affecting life, activity, etc." and ascribed to a specific time and place. And we use for "culture" the following portion of the definition: "the concepts, habits, skills, art, instruments, institutions, etc. of a given people in a given period." You can see how a climate can fit within a culture, be more changeable, and not depend on embedded technology or structures.

2. Jere E. Brophy, "Research on Self-Fulfilling Prophecy and Teacher Expectations" (Ph.D. diss., Institute for Research on Teaching, Michigan State University, 1982). Suzanne G. Scott and Reginald A. Bruce, "The Influence of Leadership, Individual Attributes and Climate on Innovative Behavior: A Model of Individual Innovation in the Workplace," *Academy of Management Journal* 37 (1994): 580–607.

3. David Welty, interview by Jeff Mauzy, tape recording, Kansas City, MO, 6 April 1999. All subsequent Welty quotes are from this interview.

4. Pete Karolczak, interview by Jeff Mauzy, tape recording, 4 June 1999. All subsequent Karolczak quotes are from this interview.

5. Peter Wesenberg, "Bridging the Individual-Social Divide: A New Perspective for Understanding and Stimulating Creativity in Organizations;" *Journal of Creative Behavior* 28, no. 3 (1994): 177–192.

6. Matt Cutler, telephone interview by Jeff Mauzy, tape recording, 22 May 2002. All subsequent Cutler quotes are from this interview.

7. Larry Bohn, telephone interview by Jeff Mauzy, tape recording, 22 May 2002. All subsequent Bohn quotes are from this interview.

8. Douglas McGregor, *The Human Side of Enterprise* (New York: McGraw Hill, 1960), 114. "The distinctive potential contribution of the human being . . . at every level of the organization, stems from his capacity to think, to plan, to exercise judgment, to be creative, to direct and to control his own behavior."

9. Edward Deci and Richard M. Ryan, "The Support of Autonomy and the Control of Behavior," *Journal of Personality and Social Psychology* 53, no. 6 (December 1987): 1024–1037. "The research review details those contextual and personal factors that tend to promote autonomy and those that tend to control and shows that autonomy support has generally been associated with more intrinsic motivation, greater interest, less pressure and tension, more creativity, more cognitive flexibility, better conceptual learning, a more positive emotional tone, higher self-esteem, more trust, greater persistence of behavior change, and better physical and psychological health than has control."

10. David Welty interview.

11. McGregor, *The Human Side of Enterprise,* 114.

CHAPTER 5

1. Carol Previte, interview by Jeff Mauzy, tape recording, Boston, MA, 22 April 1999. All subsequent Previte quotes are from this interview.

2. Darcy Bradbury, interview by Jeff Mauzy, tape recording, New York, NY, 8 September 1999. All subsequent Bradbury quotes are from this interview.

3. Marylyn Dintenfass, interview by Jeff Mauzy, tape recording, Boston, MA, 25 February 1999. All subsequent Dintenfass quotes are from this interview.

4. Rick Hensler, telephone interview by Jeff Mauzy, tape recording, 3 February 1997. All subsequent Hensler quotes are from this interview.

5. Will Novasedlik, interview by Jeff Mauzy, tape recording, Toronto, 10 February 1999.

6. Irving Kirsch, *How Expectations Shape Experience* (Washington, DC: American Psychological Association, 1999); Aaron T. Beck and Gary Emery, *Anxiety Disorders and Phobias: A Cognitive Perspective* (New York: Basic Books, 1985). People manipulate their environment until they create a situation that is in consonance with their self-image.

7. Ken Baum and Richard Trubo, *The Mental Edge: Maximize Your Sports Potential with the Mind/Body Connection* (New York: Perigee, 1999); Jack J. Lesyk, *Developing Sport Psychology within Your Clinical Practice: A Practical Guide for Mental Health Professionals* (San Francisco: Jossey-Bass, 1998), 133–142.

8. Mihaly Csikszentmihalyi, *Creativity: Flow and the Psychology of Discovery and Invention* (New York: HarperCollins, 1996), 330–331.

9. Beck and Emery, *Anxiety Disorders and Phobias,* 187, 298.

10. John Horn, "The Battle for Orlando," *Newsweek,* 12 August 2002.

11. Mark Woodbury, unrecorded observation by Jeff Mauzy, Orlando, FL, 28 February, 1997.

12. Maureen Arkle, interview by Jeff Mauzy, tape recording, Waltham, MA, 3 April 1999. Subsequent Arkle quotes are from this interview.

13. Bob Miller, interview by Jeff Mauzy, tape recording, Hauppauge, NY, 10 October 2000. All subsequent Miller quotes are from this interview.

14. Jeff Mauzy, "Managing Personal Creativity," in *Innovationsforschung und Technologie Management* (Berlin: Springer-Verlag, 1999), 26; Elizabeth Deane, interview by Jeff Mauzy, tape recording, Boston, MA, 3 April 2000.

15. Interview with Tom Peters, *Modern Maturity,* March–April 2000.

16. "How Writers Write," Geelong Small Press Publishing, <http://www.gssp.com.au/how_writers_write.htm.>

17. J. S. Adams, "Toward an Understanding of Inequity," *Journal of Abnormal and Social Psychology* 67 (1963): 422–436

CHAPTER 6

1. Kathy Lundberg, interview by Jeff Mauzy, tape recording, Palo Alto, CA, 5 March 1999. All subsequent Lundberg quotes are from this interview.

2. Beverly Mehlhoff, interview by Jeff Mauzy, tape recording, Palo Alto, CA, 5 March 1999. All subsequent Mehlhoff quotes are from this interview.

3. Emerson Martlage, interview by Jeff Mauzy, tape recording, Palo Alto, CA, 5 March 1999. All subsequent Martlage quotes are from this interview.

4. Luke Christensen, from videotape provided by Guidant, Inc., Palo Alto, CA, Winter 1998.

5. Douglas McGregor, *The Human Side of Enterprise* (New York: McGraw-Hill, 1960), 33–57.

6. Jerry McAllister, interview by Jeff Mauzy, tape recording, Minneapolis, MN, 21 February 2000. All subsequent McAllister quotes are from this interview.

7. The 3M story is pieced together from interviews with Barry Dayton, Jerry McAllister, Geoffrey Nicholson, and Mary Sonnack, all of 3M, and Eric von Hippel of MIT. Interviews with Dayton, McAllister, and Nicholson were recorded in Minneapolis, MN, 15 February 1999; interview with Sonnack was held by telephone, March 1999; interview with von Hippel was

held in February 2000. Interviews were augmented by literature provided by 3M.

8. Stephen Leichtman, interview by Jeff Mauzy, tape recording, 13 April 1999. All subsequent Leichtman quotes are from this interview.

9. Jon Kingsdale, unrecorded telephone conversation with Jeff Mauzy, February 2002.

10. Teresa M. Amabile, *Creativity in Context* (Boulder, CO: Westview Press, 1996), chapter 6; Teresa M. Amabile, "How to Kill Creativity," *Harvard Business Review,* September–October 1998, 77–87.

11. Geoffrey Nicholson, interview by Jeff Mauzy, tape recording, Minneapolis, MN, 21 February 2000. All subsequent Nicholson quotes are from this interview.

12. Amabile, *Creativity in Context,* 231–232.

13. MacArthur Fellows Program; www.macfound.org/programs/fel/fel_overview.htm.

14. Quoted in William Coyne, "Building a Tradition of Innovation," UK Innovation Lecture presented to the Royal Academy, 1996.

15. Ibid.

16. Rosabeth M. Kanter, "Three Tiers for Innovation Research," *Communication Research* 15, no. 5 (October 1998): 509–523.

17. *Business Week,* 27 August 2001. Theresa Forsman, "A Tale of Two Entrepreneurs," *Business Week* online, 22 August 2001, <http://www.businessweek.com/smallbiz/content/aug2001/sb2001/sb20010822_191.htm>; "EU must change attitude to business failures, says SMElobby," *Business Europe,* <http://uk.biz.yahoo.com/smallbus/news/finance/legal/>; Jeffrey Shuman and David Rottenberg, "Loser Chic: In the New Economy, Losers Are Winners and Failures Are Fawned Over (Well, Sometimes)," *Business Start-Ups Magazine,* February 1999; Dawn Teo, "Draper Fisher Jurvetson Sees S'pore Entrepreneurship Boom," Channel News Asia; 19 April 2001, <http://www.drapervc.com/files/timinsingapore.html>; "Phoenix Award Casts Net Wider to Recognize Entrepreneurial Risk-Takers Who Overcome Failure," press release by the Singapore Economic Development Board, together with Ernst & Young, Keppel Tatlee Bank, the Singapore Venture Capital Association, and White & Case, Colin Ng & Partners, 11 July 2001.

18. G. C. Nicholson, "Keeping Innovation Alive," *Research Technology Management,* May–June 1998, 34–40.

19. Susan Sacks, telephone interview by Jeff Mauzy, tape recording, 7 April 1999. All subsequent Sacks quotes are from this interview.

20. Isabel V. Hull, *Sexuality, State, and Civil Society in Germany, 1700–1815* (Ithaca, NY: Cornell University Press, 1996), 207–218.

21. Stuart Crainer, *The Management Century: A Critical Review of 20th Century Thought and Practice* (San Francisco: Jossey-Bass, 2000). See especially chapters 4 and 11.

22. Daniel Plankett, "The Creative Organization: An Empirical Investigation of the Importance of Participation in Decision-Making," *Journal of Creative Behavior* 24, no. 2 (1990): 140–148; M. Zuckerman et al., "On the Importance of Self-Determination for Intrinsically Motivated Behavior," *Personality and Social Psychology Bulletin* 4 (1978): 443–446.

23. Robert S. Kaplan and David P. Norton, *The Balanced Scorecard: Translating Strategy into Action* (Boston: Harvard Business School Press, 1996), 126–151.

24. Abraham Maslow, *Eupsychian Management* (Columbus, OH: Richard Irwin/McGraw-Hill, 1971), as cited in Crainer, *The Management Century,* 114.

25. Amabile, *Creativity in Context,* 135–150, 250–253. Amabile refers to a great deal of research on feedback.

26. Gordon MacKenzie, *Orbiting the Giant Hairball: A Corporate Fool's Guide to Surviving with Grace* (New York: Viking, 1996), 143–152.

27. William Dunn, unrecorded interview by Jeff Mauzy, McGaw Park, IL, 8 April 2002.

28. Sonia E. Blisset and Robert E. McGrath, "The Relationship between Creativity and Interpersonal Problem-Solving Skills in Adults;" *Journal of Creative Behavior* 30, no. 3 (1996), 173–182; Maria M. Clapham, "Ideational Skills Training: A Key Element in Creativity Training Programs," *Creativity Research Journal* 10, no. 1 (1997): 33–44; Laura H. Rose and Hsin-Tai Lin, "A meta-analysis of long-term creativity training programs," *Journal of Creative Behavior* 18, no. 1 (1984): 11–22; Nancy A. Fontenot, "Effects of Training in Creativity and Creative Problem Finding upon Business People;" *Journal of Social Psychology* 133, no. 1 (February 1993): 11–22.

29. Nitin Nohria and Nanjay Gulati, "Is Slack Good or Bad for Innovation?" *Academy of Management Journal* 39, no. 5 (October 1996): 1245–1264.

30. Raymond Miller, unrecorded telephone conversation with Jeff Mauzy, Winter 1994.

31. The Work Environment Scale by Paul M. Insel and Rudolf H. Moos helps evaluate the environment for its impact on productivity and employee satisfaction (Paul M. Insel and Rudolf H. Moos, *Work Environment Scale* [Palo Alto, CA: Consulting Psychologists Press, 1974]). Assessment instruments created by Dr. Van de Ven cover design, structures, and functions of

organizations, and how they contribute to innovation (M. S. Poole, A. Van de Ven, K. Dooley, and M. Holmes, *Organizational Change Processes: Theory and Methods for Research* [New York: Oxford University Press, 2000]). The Siegel Scale of Support of Innovation by S. Siegel and W. Kaemmerer measures support for creativity, tolerance of differences, and personal commitment (S. Siegal and W. Kaemmerer, "Measuring the Perceived Support for Innovation in Organizations," *Journal of Applied Psychology* 63 [1978]: 553–562). The KEYS survey by the Center for Creative Leadership assesses how employees perceive stimulants and barriers to creativity. The Creativity and Innovation Index by Synectics collects information on individual thinking, team interaction, and corporate support and ties the information to a company's capabilities for creativity and innovation (*The Dartmouth/Synectics Creativity and Innovation Index* [Cambridge, MA: Synectics, 2001]). Teresa M. Amabile and Nur D. Gryskiewicz, "The Creative Environment Scales: Work Environment Inventory," *Creativity Research Journal* 2, no. 4 (1989): 231–253.

32. John P. Kotter, *On What Leaders Really Do* (Boston: Harvard Business School Press, 1999), 75–93.

33. Susan Adam, telephone interview by Jeff Mauzy, tape recording, 7 January 1999.

34. Todd Sloane, unrecorded telephone interview by Jeff Mauzy, 8 February 2001.

CHAPTER 7

1. Jackie Burton, recorded observation in session by Jeff Mauzy, New York, NY, 1 August 1996. All subsequent Burton references stem from the same event.

2. Ken Olsen, President of Digital Equipment Corporation, address to the Convention of the World Future Society, Boston, 1977.

3. Jim Keene, interview by Jeff Mauzy, tape recording, Grand Rapids, MI, 20 February 1999. All subsequent Keene references are to this interview.

4. Wayne Puglia, recorded observations in session by Jeff Mauzy, Cambridge, MA, 7 June 1998. All subsequent Puglia references are to this event.

5. David Rabkin, recorded facilitated session by Jeff Mauzy, Boston, 4 November 2001. All subsequent Rabkin references are to this event.

6. Lowry Burgess, unrecorded class assignment (worked on by Jeff Mauzy), Massachusetts College of Art, 1971.

7. Harvey Ehrlich, recorded observation in session by Jeff Mauzy, Cambridge, MA, 8 August 2001.

8. ABC News, *20/20*, 13 November 1986.

9. Paul Nahass, "Web-Enabling the Stage-Gate™ Process at Albany International: Lessons Learned and Benefits Derived" (paper presented at the Web-Enabled New Product Development Conference of the Product Development and Management Association, Scottsdale, AZ, 5 December 2000), <http://www.pdma.org/vision/jul01/web-enabled2.html>.

10. John Wallingford, recorded observation in session by Jeff Mauzy, Radnor, PA, 22 March 2001.

11. Information provided by NASA (editor, spinoff magazine), MIT (technology licensing department), and Bell Labs (public relations department).

12. Randall E. Stross, "Mr. Gates Builds His Brain Trust;" *Fortune*, 8 December 1997, 84–98; "Bill Gates and Microsoft Research Chart the Future of Computing," press release from the Microsoft Corporation, Redmond, WA, 5 September 2001.

CHAPTER 8

1. Terry Egger, telephone interview by Jeff Mauzy, tape recording, 29 May 2001. All subsequent Egger quotes are from this interview.

2. Eric Steidinger, telephone interview by Jeff Mauzy, tape recording, 21 October 2001. All subsequent Steidinger quotes are from this interview.

3. Shona L. Brown and Kathleen M. Eisenhardt, *Competing on the Edge: Strategy as Structured Chaos* (Boston: Harvard Business School Press, 1998), 135–159; Michael Hammer and James Champy, *Reengineering the Corporation: A Manifesto for Business Revolution* (New York: Harper Business, 1993), 14–15, 63–64.

4. William Hamlin, telephone interview by Jeff Mauzy, tape recording, 5 December 2001. All subsequent Hamlin quotes are from this interview.

5. Mark Greiner, tape recorded interview by Jeff Mauzy, Grand Rapids, MI, 5 September 2002.

6. William Wilson, conversation with Rick Harriman, Cambridge, MA, September 1985.

7. http://www.josephsoninstitute.org/quotes/quoteindifference.htm

BIBLIOGRAPHY

INTRODUCTION

Carr, Clay. *The Competitive Power of Constant Creativity*. New York: Amacom, 1999.

Jesitus, John. "Creativity Differentiates Health Plans in Volatile, Competitive Marketplaces." *Managed Healthcare* 8, no. 6 (1988): 40–42.

Kash, Don. *Perpetual Innovation: The New World of Competition*. New York: Basic Books, 1999.

Land, George, and Beth Jarman. *Breakpoint and Beyond: Mastering the Future Today*. New York: Harper Business, 1992.

CHAPTER 1

Albert, Robert. "To Ur Is Human." *Roeper Review* 21, no. 1 (1998): 78–80.

Amabile, Teresa M. "Social Psychology of Creativity: A Componential Conceptualization." *Journal of Personality and Social Psychology* 45 (1983): 357–377.

———. "Motivation and Creativity: Effects of Motivational Orientation on Creative Writers." *Journal of Personality and Social Psychology* 48 (1985): 393–399.

———. *Growing Up Creative: Nurturing a Lifetime of Creativity*. Buffalo, NY: The Creative Education Foundation Press, 1989.

———. *Creativity in Context*. Boulder, CO: Westview Press, 1996.

———. "Entrepreneurial Creativity Through Motivational Synergy." *Journal of Creative Behavior* 31, no. 1 (1997): 18–26.

Amabile, Teresa M., and Elizabeth Tighe. "Questions of Creativity." In *Creativity, the Reality Club,* volume 4, edited by J. Brockman, 7–27. New York: Simon & Schuster, 1993.

Badsadur, Min. "Optimal Ideation-Evaluation Ratios." *Creativity Research Journal* 8, no. 1 (1995): 63–75.

Barron, Frank, Alfonso Montuori, and Andrea Barron. *Creators on Creating: Awakening and Cultivating the Imaginative Mind.* New York: G. P. Putnam, 1997.

Campbell, Donald T. "Blind Variation and Selective Retention in Creative Thought as in Other Knowledge Processes." *Psychological Review* 67, no. 6 (1960): 380–400.

Conti, Regina, Teresa M. Amabile, and Sara Pollak. "The Positive Impact of Creative Activity: Effects of Creative Task Engagement and Motivational Focus on College Students' Learning." *Personality and Social Psychology Bulletin* 21, no. 10 (1995): 1107–1116.

Csikszentmihalyi, Mihaly, and J. W. Getzels. "Creativity and Problem Finding in Art." In *The Foundations of Aesthetics, Art and Art Education,* edited by Frank H. Farley and Ronald W. Neperud, 91–116. New York: Praeger, 1998.

Czerner, Thomas B. *What Makes You Tick: The Brain in Plain English.* New York: Wiley, 2001.

Cziko, Gary A. "From Blind to Creative: In Defense of Donald Campbell's Selectionist Theory of Human Creativity." *Journal of Creative Behavior* 32, no. 3 (1998): 192–209.

Dacey, John S., and Kathleen H. Lennon. *Understanding Creativity: The Interplay of Biological, Psychological and Social Factors.* San Francisco: Jossey-Bass, 1998.

Dennett, Daniel C. *Consciousness Explained.* Boston: Little, Brown, 1991.

———. *Kinds of Minds: Toward an Understanding of Consciousness.* New York: Basic Books, 1996.

Dowling, John E. *Creating Mind: How the Brain Works.* New York: W. W. Norton, 1988.

Feldhusen, John F. "Creativity: A Knowledge Base, Metacognitive Skills, and Personality Factors." *Journal of Creative Behavior* 29, no. 4 (1995): 225–268.

Finke, Ronald A., Thomas B. Ward, and Steven M. Smith. *Creative Cognition: Theory, Research and Application.* Cambridge, MA: MIT Press, 1996.

Ford, Donna Y., and J. John Harris. "The Elusive Definition of Creativity." *Journal of Creative Behavior* 26, no. 3 (1992): 186–198.

Fritz, Robert. *The Path of Least Resistance: Learning to Become the Creative Force in Your Own Life*. Expanded edition. New York: Fawcett Books, 1989.

Gardner, Howard. *Intelligence Reframed: Multiple Intelligences for the 21st Century*. New York: Basic Books, 1999.

Gardner, Howard, and Emma Policastro. "From Case Studies to Robust Generalizations: An Approach to the Study of Creativity." *Handbook of Creativity*, edited by Robert J. Sternberg, 213–225. New York: Cambridge University Press, 1999.

Getzels, J. W. "Problem Finding and the Inventiveness of Solutions." *Journal of Creative Behavior* 9, no. 1 (1975): 12–18.

———. "Problem Finding: A Theoretical Note." *Cognitive Science* 3 (1979): 167–172.

Ghislelin, Brewster. *The Creative Process: Reflections on Invention in the Arts and Sciences*. Berkeley: University of California Press, 1952.

Gray, Jeffrey A., and Neil McNaughton. "The Neuropsychology of Anxiety: Reprise." In *Nebraska Symposium on Motivation, 1995: Perspectives on Anxiety, Panic and Fear, Current Theory and Research in Motivation*, 43 (1996): 61–134.

Hyman, Steven E. "Briefing on the Brain-Body Connection." Paper presented to the U.S. House of Representatives, Subcommittee on Labor, DHHS, Education and Related Agencies, Washington, DC, 5 November 1977.

Isaksen, Scott, and Gerard J. Puccio. "Adaptation-Innovation and the Torrance Tests of Creative Thinking: The Level-Style Issue Revisited." *Psychological Reports* 63, no. 2 (1988): 659–670.

Jausovec, N. "Metacognition in Creative Problem-Solving." In *Problem Finding, Problem Solving and Creativity*, edited by Mark Runco, 77–95. Norwood, NJ: Ablex, 1992.

Kitchener, K. S. "Cognition, Meta-Cognition and Epistemic Cognition." *Human Development* 26 (1983): 222–232.

Knowles, Brian. "What Managers Can Learn from Artists about Creativity." In *Handbook for Creative and Innovative Managers*, edited by Robert Lawrence Kuhn, 61–66. New York: McGraw-Hill, 1988.

Koestler, Arthur. *The Act of Creation*. New York: Macmillan, 1964.

Kosslyn, Stephen M., and Olivier Koenig. *Wet Mind: The New Cognitive Neuroscience*. New York: Free Press, 1995.

Maier, N. R., and A. R. Solem. "Improving Solutions by Turning Choice Situations into Problems." In *Problem Solving and Creativity: In Individuals and Groups*, edited by N. R. Maier, 390–395. Belmont, CA: Brooks/Cole, 1970.

McAleer, Neil. "The Roots of Inspiration." *Creative Management,* edited by Jane Henry, 12–15. Milton Keynes, England: Open University Press, 1991.

Obiols, Jordi E. "Art and Creativity: Neuropsychological Perspectives." In *Depression and the Spiritual in Modern Art: Homage to Miro,* edited by Joseph Schildkraut and Aurora Otero, 33–47. New York: Wiley, 1996.

Okebukola, Peter A. "Relationships among Anxiety Belief Systems and Creativity." *Journal of Social Psychology* 126, no. 6 (1986): 815–816.

Perkins, David N. "Creativity and the Quest for Mechanism." In *The Psychology of Thought,* edited by R. J. Sternberg and E. E. Smith, 309–336. New York: Cambridge University Press, 1988.

Perkins, Daniel N. *The Mind's Best Work.* Cambridge, MA: Harvard University Press, 1981.

Peterson, J. B. *Maps of Meaning: The Architecture of Belief.* New York: Routledge, 1999.

Reisberg, Daniel. *Cognition: Exploring the Science of the Mind.* New York: W. W. Norton, 1997.

Rose, Gilbert J. *Trauma and Mastery in Life and Art.* New Haven, CT: Yale University Press, 1987.

Runco, Mark A. "Implicit Theories and Ideational Creativity." In *Theories of Creativity,* edited by M. A. Runco and R. S. Albert, 234–252. Newbury Park, CA: Sage Publications, Inc., 1990.

Schneider, Susan. "Learning to Be Creative." *American Psychologist* 52, no. 7 (1997): 745.

Schuldberg, David. "Giddiness and Horror in the Creative Process." In *Creativity and Affect,* edited by Melvin Shaw and Mark Runco, 87–101. Norwood, NJ: Ablex, 1994.

Shanteau, James, and Geri Anne Dino. "Environmental Stressor Effects on Creativity and Decision Making." In *Time Pressure and Stress in Human Judgment and Decision Making,* edited by Ola Svenson and A. John Maule, 293–308. New York: Plenum Press, 1993.

Simonton, Dean Keith. "Political Pathology and Societal Creativity." *Creativity Research Journal* 3, no. 2 (1990): 85–99.

———. "Creativity in Personality, Developmental and Social Psychology: Any Links with Cognitive Psychology?" In *Creative Thought: An Investigation of Conceptual Structures and Processes,* edited by Thomas Ward and Steven M. Smith, 309–324. Washington, DC: American Psychological Association, 1997.

Sternberg, Robert J. "Cognitive Mechanisms in Human Creativity: Is Variation Blind or Sighted?" *Journal of Creative Behavior* 32, no. 3 (1998): 159–176.

———, ed. *Handbook of Creativity*. New York: Cambridge University Press, 1999.

Taylor, Irving A., and J. W. Getzels. *Perspectives in Creativity*. Chicago, IL: Aldine, 1975.

Van der Kolk, B. A. "The Body Keeps the Score: Memory and the Emerging Psychobiology of Post-Traumatic Stress." *Harvard Review of Psychiatry* 1, no. 5 (1994): 253–265.

Zdep, S. M. "Intelligence, Creativity and Anxiety among College Students." *Psychological Reports* 19 (1966): 420.

CHAPTER 2

Abra, Jock C. "Competition: Creativity's Vilified Motive." *Genetic, Social and General Psychology Monographs* 119, no. 3 (1993): 289–342.

Albert, Robert. "Some Reasons Why Childhood Creativity Often Fails to Make It Past Puberty into the Real World." In *Creativity from Childhood Through Adulthood: The Developmental Issues: New Directions for Child Development*, edited by Mark A. Runco, 43–56. San Francisco, CA: Jossey-Bass, 1996.

Barlow, David H., and Michelle G. Craske. *Mastery of Your Anxiety and Panic II*. New York: Graywind Publications, 1994.

Borysenko, Joan. *Minding the Body, Mending the Mind*. New York: Bantam, 1988.

Csikszentmihalyi, Mihaly. *Creativity: Flow and the Psychology of Discovery and Invention*. New York: Harper Collins, 1996.

Edstrom, Jennifer, and Marlin Ellen. *Barbarians Led by Bill Gates: Microsoft from the Inside*. New York: Henry Holt, 1998.

Hennessey, Beth A., Teresa M. Amabile, and Margaret Martinage. "Immunizing Children against the Negative Effects of Reward." *Contemporary Educational Psychology* 14, no. 3 (1989): 212–227.

Matthews, Gerald. "The Effects of Anxiety on Intellectual Performance: When and Why Are They Found." *Journal of Research in Personality* 20 (1986): 385–401.

Mauzy, Jeffrey H. "Managing Personal Creativity." In *Innovationforschung und Technologiemanagement*, edited by Franke/von Braun, 20–31. Berlin: Springer-Verlag, 1999.

May, Rollo. *The Courage to Create*. New York: W. W. Norton, 1994.

O'Neill, Sharon, and Daniel Shallcross. "Sensational Thinking: A Teaching/Learning Model for Creativity." *Journal of Creative Behavior* 28, no. 2 (1994): 75–88.

Rickards, Tudor. "Creative Leadership: Messages from the Front Line and the Back Room." *Journal of Creative Behavior* 27, no. 1 (1993): 46–56.

Sun Tzu. *The Art of War*. Translated by James Clavell. London: Hodder & Stoughton, 1981.

Torrance, E. Paul. "Can We Teach Children to Think Creatively?" *Journal of Creative Behavior* 6, no. 2 (1972): 114–143.

White, Kinnard. "Anxiety, Extraversion-Introversion, and Divergent Thinking Ability." *Journal of Creative Behavior* 2, no. 2 (1968): 119–127.

CHAPTER 3

Amason, Allen C., Kenneth R. Thompson, Wayne A. Hochwarter, and Allison W. Harrison. "An Important Dimension in Successful Management Teams." *Organizational Dynamics* 24, no. 2 (1995): 20–35.

Ambrose, Don. "Creatively Intelligent Post-Industrial Organizations and Intellectually Impaired Bureaucracies." *Journal of Creative Behavior* 29, no. 1 (1995): 1–15.

Carnevale, Peter J., and Tahira M. Probst. "Good News About Competitive People." In *Using Conflict in Organizations,* edited by Carsten K. De Dreu and Evert Van de Vliert, 129–146. London: Sage Publications, 1997.

Christensen, Clayton M. *The Innovator's Dilemma: When New Technologies Cause Great Firms to Fail*. Boston: Harvard Business School Press, 1997.

Clapham, Maria M. "Ideational Skills Training: A Key Element in Creativity Training Programs." *Creativity Research Journal* 10, no. 1 (1997): 33–44.

Claxton, Guy. "Investigating Human Intuition: Knowing Without Knowing Why." *Psychologist* 11, no. 5 (1998): 217–220.

De Dreu, Carsten. "Productive Conflict: The Importance of Conflict Management and Conflict Issues." In *Using Conflict in Organizations,* edited by Carsten K. De Dreu and Evert Van de Vliert, 9–22. London: Sage Publications, 1997.

Fodor, Eugene M., and Dianne Roffe-Steinrotter. "Rogerian Leadership Style and Creativity." *Journal of Research in Personality* 32, no. 2 (1998): 236–242.

Fontenot, Nancy A. "Effects of Training in Creativity and Creative Problem Finding upon Business People." *Journal of Social Psychology* 133, no. 1 (1993): 11–22.

Grossman, Stephen. "Training Creativity and Creative Problem Solving." *Training and Development Journal* 36 (1982): 62–68.

Hennessey, Beth A., and Teresa M. Amabile. "The Conditions of Creativity" In *The Nature of Creativity: Contemporary Psychological Perspectives,* edited by Robert J. Sternberg, 11–38. New York: Cambridge University Press, 1988.

Hirshberg, Jerry. *The Creative Priority: Driving Innovative Business in the Real World.* New York: Harper Business, 1998.

James, Keith. "Goal Conflict and Originality of Thinking." *Creativity Research Journal* 8, no. 3 (1995): 285–290.

James, Keith, Julie Chen, and Catherine Goldberg. "Organizational Conflict and Individual Creativity." *Journal of Applied Psychology* 22, no. 7 (1992): 545–566.

Kabanoff, Boris, and Preston Bottger. "Effectiveness of Creativity Training and Its Relation to Selected Personality Factors." *Journal of Organizational Behavior* 12 (1991): 235–248.

Kilmek, Mark, and Nate Hardcastle. "How Winners Do It." *Forbes,* 24 August 1998, 88–92.

Kolb, Judith. "Leadership of Creative Teams." *Journal of Creative Behavior* 26, no. 1 (1992): 1–9.

Mumford, Michael D., and Sigrid B. Gustafson. "Creativity Syndrome: Integration, Application and Innovation." *Psychological Bulletin* 103, no. 1 (1988): 27–43.

Nathan, Richard. "NEC Organizing for Creativity, Nimbleness." *Research Technology Management* 41, no. 4 (1998): 1–4.

Nemeth, Charlan Jeanne. "Dissent as Driving Cognition, Attitudes and Judgment." *Social Cognition* 13, no. 3 (1995): 273–291.

Parnes, Sidney J., and Arnold Meadow. "Effects of 'Brainstorming' Instructions on Creative Problem Solving by Trained and Untrained Subjects." *Journal of Educational Psychology* 50, no. 4 (1959): 171–176.

Rose, Laura H., and Hsin-tai Lin. "A Meta-Analysis of Long-Term Creativity Training Programs." *Journal of Creative Behavior* 18, no. 1 (1984): 11–22.

Shalley, Christina E., and Greg R. Oldham. "Competition and Creative Performance: Effects of Competitor Presence and Visibility." *Creativity Research Journal* 10, no. 4 (1997): 337–345.

Sheldon, Kennon M. "Creativity and Goal Conflict." *Creativity Research Journal* 8, no. 3 (1995): 299–306.

Treffinger, Donald J., and John Curtis Gowan. "An Updated Representative List of Methods and Educational Programs for Stimulating Creativity." *Journal of Creative Behavior* 5, no. 2 (1971): 127–139.

Turner, Marlene E., and Anthony R. Pratkanis. "Mitigating Groupthink by Simulating Constructive Conflict." In *Using Conflict in Organizations,* edited by Carsten K. De Dreu and Evert Van de Vliert, 53–71. London: Sage Publications, Inc., 1997.

von Hippel, Eric, Stefan Thomke, and Mary Sonnack. "Creating Break-throughs at 3M." *Harvard Business Review,* September–October 1999, 47–57.

CHAPTER 4

Amabile, Teresa M., Phyllis Goldfarb, and Shereen C. Brackfield. "Social Influences on Creativity: Evaluation, Coaction and Surveillance." *Creativity Research Journal* 3, no. 1 (1990): 6–21.

Bennis, Warren, and Patricia Ward Biederman. *Organizing Genius: The Secrets of Creative Collaboration.* Cambridge, MA: Perseus, 1997.

Blackwell, Dick. "Bounded Instability, Group Analysis and the Matrix: Organizations Under Stress." *Group Analysis* 31, no. 4 (1998): 532–546.

Burnside, Robert M. "Improving Corporate Climates for Creativity." In *Innovation and Creativity at Work: Psychological and Organizational Strategies,* edited by Michael A. West and James L. Farr, 265–284. Chichester, England: Wiley, 1990.

Chatman, Jennifer A., Jeffrey T. Polzer, Sigal G. Barsade, and Margaret A. Neale. "Being Different Yet Feeling Similar: The Influence of Demographic Composition and Organizational Culture on Work Processes and Outcomes." *Administrative Science Quarterly* 43, no. 4 (1998): 749–780.

Csikszentmihalyi, Mihaly. "Creativity and Genius: A Systems Perspective." In *Genius and Mind: Studies of Creativity and Temperament,* edited by Andrew Steptoe, 39–64. New York: Oxford University Press, 1988.

Deci, Edward L., and Richard M. Ryan. "The Support of Autonomy and the Control of Behavior." *Journal of Personality and Social Psychology* 53, no. 6 (1987): 1024–1037.

Estrada, Carlos A., Alice M. Isen, and Mark J. Young. "Positive Affect Improves Creative Problem Solving and Influences Reported Source of Practice Satisfaction in Physicians." *Motivation and Emotion* 18, no. 4 (1994): 285–299.

Ferguson, Tim W. "Who's Mentoring Whom?" *Forbes,* 19 May 1997, 253.

Fitzpatrick, Sheila. *The Russian Revolution.* London: Oxford University Press, 1994.

Greene, Terry B., and Helga Noice. "Influence of Positive Affect upon Creative Thinking and Problem Solving in Children." *Psychological Reports* 63 (1988): 895–898.

Hammerschmidt, Peter K. "The Kirton Adaptation Innovation Inventory and Group Problem Solving Success Rate." *Journal of Creative Behavior* 30, no. 1 (1996): 61–74.

Isen, Alice M., Kimberly A. Daubman, and Gary P. Nowicki. "Positive Affect Facilitates Creative Problem Solving." *Journal of Personality and Social Psychology* 52, no. 6 (1987): 1122–1131.

Kanter, Rosabeth Moss. "Ourselves versus Ourselves." *Harvard Business Review,* May–July 1992, 8–10.

Kolb, Deborah M., and Priscilla A. Glidden. "Getting to Know Your Conflict Options: Using Conflict as a Creative Force." *Personnel Administrator* 31, no. 6 (1986): 77–90.

Runco, Mark A. "Creativity and Its Discontents." In *Creativity and Affect: Creativity Research,* edited by Melvin Shaw and Mark Runco, 102–123. Norwood, NJ: Ablex, 1994.

Schneider, Benjamin. "Organizational Behavior." *Annual Review of Psychology* 36 (1985): 573–611.

Scott, Suzanne G., and Reginald A. Bruce. "The Influence of Leadership, Individual Attributes and Climate on Innovative Behavior: A Model of Individual Innovation in the Workplace." *Academy of Management Journal* 37 (1994): 580–607.

Staw, Barry M. "An Evolutionary Approach to Creativity and Innovation." In *Innovation and Creativity at Work: Psychological and Organizational Strategies,* edited by Michael A. West and James L. Farr, 287–308. Chichester, England: Wiley, 1990.

Tesluk Paul E., James L. Farr, and Stephanie R. Klein. "Influences of Organizational Culture and Climate on Individual Creativity." *Journal of Creative Behavior* 31, no. 1 (1997): 27–41.

Wesenberg, Peter. "Bridging the Individual-Social Divide: A New Perspective for Understanding and Stimulating Creativity in Organizations." *Journal of Creative Behavior* 28, no. 3 (1994): 177–192.

West, Michael A. "The Social Psychology of Innovation in Groups." In *Innovation and Creativity at Work: Psychological and Organizational Strategies,* edited by Michael A. West and James L. Farr, 309–333. Chichester, England: Wiley, 1990.

Woodman, Richard, John E. Sawyer, and Ricky W. Riffin. "Toward a Theory of Organizational Creativity." *Academy of Management Review* 18, no. 2 (1993): 293–321.

CHAPTER 5

Adams, J. S. "Toward an Understanding of Inequity." *Journal of Abnormal and Social Psychology* 67 (1963): 422–436.

Amabile, Teresa M., and R. Conti. "Changes in the Work Environment for Creativity During Downsizing." *Academy of Management Journal* 42, no. 6 (1999): 630–640.

Buzan, Tony. *Use Your Head*. London: BBC Publications, 1974.

———. *The Brain Users Guide*. New York: E. P. Dutton, 1983.

Scott, Mary E. "How Stress Can Affect Gifted/Creative Potential: Ideas to Better Insure Realization of Potential." *Creative Child and Adult Quarterly* 10, no. 4 (1985): 240–249.

Vaillant, George E. *Adaptation to Life*. Boston: Little, Brown, 1977.

CHAPTER 6

Adler, Seymour, and Howard M. Weiss. "Criterion Aggregation in Personality Research: A Demonstration Looking at Self-Esteem and Goal Setting." *Human Performance* 1, no. 2 (1988): 99–109.

Amabile, Teresa M. "Effects of External Evaluation on Artistic Creativity." *Journal of Personality and Social Psychology* 37 (1979): 221–233.

———. "From Individual Creativity to Organizational Innovation." In *Innovation: A Cross-Disciplinary Perspective,* edited by Kjell Gronhaug and Geir Kaufmann, 139–166. Oslo, Norway: Norwegian University Press, 1988.

Amabile, Teresa M., and Nur D. Gryskiewicz. "The Creative Environment Scales: Work Environment Inventory." *Creativity Research Journal* 2, no. 4 (1989): 231–253.

Amabile, Teresa M., Beth A. Hennessey, and Barbara S. Grossman. "Social Influences on Creativity: The Effects of Contracted-For Reward." *Journal of Personality and Social Psychology* 50, no. 1 (1986): 14–23.

Amabile, Teresa M., Regina Conti, Heather Coon, and Jeffrey Lazenby. "Assessing the Work Environment for Creativity." *Academy of Management Journal* 39, no. 5 (1996): 1154–1184.

Arad, Sharon, Mary Ann Hanson, and Robert J. Schneider. "A Framework for the Study of Relationships Between Organizational Characteristics and Organizational Innovation." *Journal of Creative Behavior* 31, no. 1 (1997): 42–58.

Baer, John. "Divergent Thinking Is Not a General Trait: A Multidomain Training Experiment." *Creativity Research Journal* 7, no. 1 (1994): 35–46.

Bailyn, Lotte. "Autonomy in the Industrial R&D Lab." *Human Resource Management* 24, no. 2 (1985): 129–146.

Bartlett, Christopher A., and Afroze Mohammed. "3M: Profile of an Innovating Company." Case 9-395-016. Boston: Harvard Business School, 1995.

Carson, Paula P., and Kerry D. Carson. "Managing Creativity Enhancement Through Goal-Setting and Feedback." *Journal of Creative Behavior* 27, no. 1 (1993): 36–45.

Cooper, Robert, K., and Ayman Sawaf. *Executive EQ: Emotional Intelligence in Leadership and Organizations.* New York: Grosset/Putnam, 1996.

Coyne, William. "Building a Tradition of Innovation." UK Innovation Lecture, The Royal Society, London, 1996.

Deci, Edward L., and Richard M. Ryan. "Human Autonomy: The Basis for True Self-Esteem." In *Efficacy, Agency and Self-Esteem,* edited by Michael H. Kernis, 31–49. New York: Plenum Press, 1995.

Dougherty, Deborah, and Cynthia Hardy. "Sustained Product Innovation in Large, Mature Organizations: Overcoming Innovation-to-Organization Problems." *Academy of Management Journal* 39, no. 5 (1996): 1120–1153.

Duchon, Dennis. "Is It Possible to Manage Creativity with Goal Setting?" *Journal of Human Behavior and Learning* 6, no. 1 (1989): 50–61.

Gibson, Fredrick W., Fred E. Feidler, and Kelley M. Barrett. "Stress, Babble and the Utilization of the Leader's Intellectual Abilities." *Leadership Quarterly* 4, no. 2 (1993): 189–208.

Greenberg, Ellen. "Creativity, Autonomy, and Evaluation of Creative Work: Artistic Workers in Organizations." *Journal of Creative Behavior* 26, no. 2 (1992): 75–80.

Gundry, Lisa, Jill Kickul, and Charles Prather. "Building the Creative Organization." *Organizational Dynamics* 22, no. 4 (1994): 22–37.

Hage, J., and R. Dewar. "Elite Values versus Organizational Structure in Predicting Innovation." *Administrative Science Quarterly* 18 (1973): 279–290.

Hennessey, Beth A. "Toward an Educational Psychology of Creativity: Comment and Reflection." *Educational Psychological Review* 7, no. 2 (1995): 209–213.

Hennessey, Beth A., and Teresa M. Amabile. "Reality, Intrinsic Motivation and Creativity." *American Psychologist* 53, no. 6 (1998): 574–575.

Hequet, Marc. "Doing More with Less." *Training* 32 (1985): 76–82.

Hull, Isabel V. *Sexuality, State, and Civil Society in Germany, 1700–1815.* Ithaca, New York: Cornell University Press, 1996.

Insel, Paul M., and Rudolf H. Moos. *Work Environment Scale.* Palo Alto, CA: Consulting Psychologists Press, 1974.

Kanter, Rosabeth Moss. "Three Tiers for Innovation Research." *Communication Research* 15, no. 5 (1988): 509–523.

————. "When a Thousand Flowers Bloom: Structural, Collective and Social Conditions for Innovation in Organizations." *Research in Organizational Behavior* 10 (1988): 169–211.

Kohn, Alfie. "Why Incentive Plans Cannot Work." *Harvard Business Review,* September–October 1993, reprint 93506.

————. "Rethinking Rewards." *Harvard Business Review,* November–December 1993, reprint 93610.

Kuczmarski, Thomas D. *Innovation: Leadership Strategies for the Competitive Edge.* Lincolnwood, IL: NTC Business Books, 1996.

Maslow, Abraham. *Toward a Psychology of Being.* 3d ed. New York: Wiley, 1998.

McGregor, Douglas. *The Human Side of Enterprise.* New York: McGraw-Hill, 1960.

Mehr, David G., and Phillip R. Shaver. "Goal Structures in Creative Motivation." *Journal of Creative Behavior* 30, no. 2 (1996): 77–104.

Monge, Peter R., Michael D. Cozzens, and Noshir S. Contractor. "Communication and Motivational Predictors of the Dynamics of Organizational Innovation." *Organization Science* 3, no. 2 (1992): 250–274.

Nicholson, G. C. "Keeping Innovation Alive." *Research Technology Management,* May–June 1998, 34–40.

Nicotera, Anne M., Michael Smilowitz, and Judy C. Pearson. "Ambiguity Tolerance, Conflict Management, Style and Argumentativeness as Predictors of Innovativeness." *Communication Research Reports* 7, no. 2 (1990): 125–131.

Nohria, Nitin, and Ranjay Gulati. "Is Slack Good or Bad for Innovation?" *Academy of Management Journal* 39, no. 5 (1996): 1245–1264.

Parker, R. C. *The Management of Innovation.* New York: Wiley, 1992.

Plunkett, Daniel. "The Creative Organization: An Empirical Investigation of the Importance of Participation in Decision-Making." *Journal of Creative Behavior* 24, no. 2 (1990): 140–148.

Pollick, Michael F., and V. K. Kumar. "Creativity Styles of Supervising Managers." *Journal of Creative Behavior* 31, no. 4 (1997) 260–270.

Poole, M. S., A. Van de Ven, K. Dooley, and M. Holmes. *Organizational Change Processes: Theory and Methods for Research.* New York: Oxford University Press, 2000.

Rausdepp, Eugene. "Establishing a Creative Climate." *Training and Development* 41, no. 4 (1987): 50–53.

Ray, Darrel W. "How to Be an Idea Generator." *Training and Development* 39, no. 1 (1985): 44–47.

Redmond, Matthew R., Michael D. Mumford, and Richard Teach. "Putting Creativity to Work: Effects of Leader Behavior on Subordinate Creativity." *Organizational Behavior & Human Decision Processes 55,* no. 1 (1993): 120–151.

Ryan, Kathleen D., and Daniel K. Oestreich. *Driving Fear Out of the Workplace: Creating the High-Trust, High-Performance Organization.* San Francisco, CA: Jossey-Bass, 1988.

Scott, Susanne G., and Reginald A. Bruce. "Determinants of Innovative Behavior: A Path Model of Individual Innovation in the Workplace." *Academy of Management Journal* 37, no. 3 (1994): 580–607.

Shalley, Christina E. "Effects of Coaction, Expected Evaluation and Goal Setting on Creativity and Productivity." *Academy of Management Journal* 38, no. 2 (1995): 483–503.

Shaw, Gordon, Robert Brown, and Philip Bromiley. "Strategic Stories: How 3M is Rewriting Business Planning." *Harvard Business Review,* May–June 1998, 41–50.

Siegal, S., and W. Kaemmerer. "Measuring the Perceived Support for Innovation in Organizations." *Journal of Applied Psychology* 63 (1978): 553–562.

Sosik, John J., Surinder S. Kahai, and Bruce J. Avolio. "Transformational Leadership and Dimensions of Creativity: Motivating Idea Generation in Computer-Mediated Groups." *Creativity Research Journal* 11, no. 2 (1998): 111–121.

Synectics. *The Dartmouth/Synectics Creativity and Innovation Index.* Cambridge, MA: Synectics, Inc., 2000.

Williams, Wendy, and Lana Yang. "Organizational Creativity." In *Handbook of Creativity,* edited by Robert J. Sternberg, 373–391. New York: Cambridge University Press, 1999.

Yong, Leonard M. S. "Managing Creative People." *Journal of Creative Behavior* 28, no. 1 (1994): 16–20.

Zhou, Jing. "Feedback Valence, Feedback Style, Task Autonomy and Achievement Orientation: Interactive Effects on Creative Performance." *Journal of Applied Psychology* 83, no. 2 (1998): 261–276.

CHAPTER 7

Ackoff, Rossell L., and Elsa Vergara. "Creativity in Problem Solving and Planning: A Review." *European Journal of Operational Research* 7 (1981): 1–13.

Badsadur, Min, Mitsuru Wakabayashi, and George Graen. "Individual Problem-Solving Styles and Attitudes Toward Divergent Thinking Before and After Training." *Creativity Research Journal* 3, no. 1 (1990): 22–32.

Begley, Sharon. "The Houses of Innovation." *Newsweek,* 22 December 1997.

Billington, Jim. "Customer-Driven Innovation." *Harvard Management Update,* July 1998, 7–9.

Blissett, Sonia E., and Robert E. McGrath. "The Relationship Between Creativity and Interpersonal Problem-Solving Skills in Adults." *Journal of Creative Behavior* 30, no. 3 (1996): 173–182.

Ceserani, Jonne, and Peter Greatwood. *Innovation and Creativity: Getting Ideas, Developing Solutions, Winning Commitment.* London: Kogan Page Limited, 1995.

De Bono, Edward. *Serious Creativity: Using the Power of Lateral Thinking to Create New Ideas.* New York: Harper Business, 1992.

Einstein, A., and L. Infeld. *The Evolution of Physics.* New York: Simon & Schuster, 1938.

Gordon, William J. J. *Synetics: The Development of Creative Capacity.* New York: Harper & Row, 1961.

Hargadon, Andrew, and Robert Sutton. "Technology Brokering and Innovation in a Product Development Firm." *Administrative Science Quarterly* 42, no. 4 (1997): 716–749.

Isaksen, Scott. "Toward a Model for the Facilitation of Creative Problem Solving." *Journal of Creative Behavior* 17, no. 1 (1983): 18–31.

Maier, N. R., and R. A. Maier. "An Experimental Test of the Effects of 'Developmental' versus 'Free' Discussion on the Quality of Groups' Decisions." In *Problem Solving and Creativity: In Individuals and Groups,* edited by N. R. Maier, 253–258. Belmont, CA: Brooks/Cole, 1970.

Nolan, Vincent. *The Innovator's Handbook: The Skills of Innovative Management: Problem Solving, Communicating, and Teamwork.* New York: Penguin Books, 1989.

Pesut, Daniel. "Creative Thinking as a Self-Regulatory Metacognitive Process—A Model for Education, Training and Further Research." *Journal of Creative Behavior* 24, no. 2 (1990): 105–110.

Prince, George M. *Practice of Creativity: A Manual for Dynamic Group Problem Solving.* New York: Harper & Row, 1970.

Sosik, John J., Bruce J. Avolio, and Surinder S. Kahai. "Inspiring Group Creativity: Comparing Anonymous and Identified Electronic Brainstorming." *Small Group Research* 29, no. 1 (1998): 3–31.

Thompson, Timothy N. "Dialectics, Communication, and Exercises for Creativity." *Journal of Creative Behavior* 25, no. 1 (1991): 43–51.

Thornburg, Thomas. "Group Size & Member Diversity Influence on Creative Performance." *Journal of Creative Behavior* 25, no. 4 (1991): 324–333.

Valery, Nicholas. "Survey: Innovation in Industry: Leaps of Faith." *The Economist,* 20 February 1999, 5–28.

Weber, Robert J., and David N. Perkins. "How to Invent Artifacts and Ideas." *New Ideas in Psychology* 7, no. 1 (1989): 49–72.

West, Michael A., and Neil R. Anderson. "Innovation in Top Management Teams." *Journal of Applied Psychology* 81, no. 6 (1996): 680–693.

CHAPTER 8

Austin, John R. "A Cognitive Framework for Understanding Demographic Influences in Groups." *The International Journal of Organizational Analysis* 5, no. 4 (1997): 342–359.

Brand, Stewart. *The Media Lab: Inventing the Future at MIT.* New York: Penguin, 1987.

Conway, Edel, and John McMackin. "Developing a Culture for Innovation: What Is the Role of the HR System?" *Dublin University Business School Research Papers* 32 (1997–1998), <http://www.dcu.ie/business/research_paper/no.32.html>.

Kanter, Rosabeth Moss. *The Change Masters: Innovation and Entrepreneurship in the American Corporation.* New York: Simon & Schuster, 1983.

———. "Mastering Change: The Skills We Need." In *Not as Far As You Think: The Realities of Working Women,* edited by L. Moore. Lexington, MA: Lexington Books, 1985.

Kotter, John P. *John P. Kotter on What Leaders Really Do.* Boston: Harvard Business School Press, 1999.

Nathan, Richard. "Spinoff to Market Technology from NEC Research Institute." *Research Technology Management,* January–February 1998.

Senge, Peter. *The Fifth Discipline: The Art and Practice of the Learning Organization.* New York: Doubleday, 1994.

Senge, Peter, Art Kleiner, Charlotte Roberts, Rick Ross, George Roth, and Bryan Smith. *The Dance of Change: The Challenges of Sustaining Momentum in a Learning Organization.* New York: Doubleday, 1999.

Sharma, Anurag. "Central Dilemmas of Managing Innovation in Large Firms." *California Management Review* 41, no. 3 (1999): 146–161.

Smith, Douglas K. *Taking Charge of Change: 10 Principles for Managing People and Performance.* Reading, MA: Addison-Wesley, 1996.

Stephenson, Karen. "Interview: Karen Stephenson." *Journal of Property Management* 63, no. 6 (1998): 10–12.

Van de Ven, Andrew, and Marshall Scott Poole. "Explaining Development and Change in Organizations." *Academy of Management Review,* July 1995.

GENERAL

Albert, Robert. "Real-World Creativity and Eminence: An Enduring Relationship." *Creativity Research Journal* 3, no. 1 (1990): 1–5.

Amabile, Teresa M. "How to Kill Creativity." *Harvard Business Review,* September–October 1998, 77–87.

Charnes, A., and W. W. Cooper, eds. *Creative and Innovative Management: Essays in Honor of George Kozmetsky.* Cambridge, MA: Ballinger, 1984.

Collins, James C., and Jerry I. Porras. *Built to Last: Successful Habits of Visionary Companies.* New York: Harper Business, 1994.

Cooper, Eileen. "A Critique of Six Measures for Assessing Creativity." *Journal of Creative Behavior* 25, no. 3 (1991): 194–204.

Cramond, Bonnie. "The Torrance Tests of Creative Thinking: From Design Through Establishment of Predictive Validity." In *Beyond Terman: Contemporary Longitudinal Studies of Giftedness and Talent,* edited by Rena Faye Subotnik and Karen D. Arnold, 229–254. Norwood, NJ: Ablex, 1994.

Dentler, Robert A., and Bernard Mackler. "Originality: Some Social and Personal Determinants." *Behavioral Science* 9 (1964): 194–204.

Engle, Diedre E., Joe J. Mah, and Golnaz Sadri. "An Empirical Comparison of Entrepreneurs and Employees: Implications for Innovation." *Creativity Research Journal* 10, no. 1 (1997): 45–49.

Fernald, Lloyd W. "The Underlying Relationship Between Creativity, Innovation, and Entrepreneurship." *Journal of Creative Behavior* 22, no. 3 (1998): 196–202.

Fleenor, John W., and Sylvester Taylor. "Construct Validity of Three Self-Report Measures of Creativity." *Educational and Psychological Measurements* 54, no. 2 (1994): 464–470.

Foster, Richard. *Innovation: The Attacker's Advantage.* New York: Summit Books, 1986.

Gadzella, Bernadette M., and Elizabeth Penland. "Is Creativity Related to Scores on Critical Thinking?" *Psychological Reports* 77, no. 3 (1995): 817–818.

Gardner, Howard. "Creativity: An Interdisciplinary Perspective." *Creativity Research Journal* 1 (1988): 8–26.

Goldstein, Joseph. *The Experience of Insight: A Simple and Direct Guide to Buddhist Meditation.* Boston: Shambhala Publications, 1976.

Goleman, Daniel P. *Emotional Intelligence: Why It Can Matter More Than IQ.* New York: Bantam, 1995.

Goleman, Daniel P., Paul Kaufman, and Michael Ray. *The Creative Spirit.* New York: Penguin Books, 1992.

Hamel, Gary, and C. K. Prahalad. *Competing for the Future: Breakthrough Strategies for Seizing Control of Your Industry and Creating the Markets of Tomorrow.* Boston: Harvard Business School Press, 1994.

Harvard Business Review. *Harvard Business Review on Change.* Boston: Harvard Business School Press, 1991.

———. *Harvard Business Review on Breakthrough Thinking.* Boston: Harvard Business School Press, 1999.

Isaksen, Scott G., and Geir Kaufmann. "Adaptors and Innovators: Different Perceptions of the Psychological Climate for Creativity." *Studia Psychologica* 32, no. 2 (1990): 129–141.

Jarrett, James L. "Personality and Artistic Creativity." *Journal of Aesthetic Education* 22, no. 4 (1998): 21–29.

Kanter, Rosabeth Moss, John Kao, and Fred Wiersma. *Innovation: Breakthrough Thinking at 3M, DuPont, GE, Pfizer, and Rubbermaid.* New York: Harper Business, 1997.

Kets de Vries, M. F. R. "Leadership for Creativity: Generating Peak Experiences." Working paper 1996/62, INSEAD, Fontainebleau, France, 1996.

Kiely, Thomas. "The Idea Makers." *Technology Review* 96 (1993): 32–40.

Kimberly, J. R., and M. J. Evanisko. "Organizational Innovation: The Influence of Individual, Organizational, and Contextual Factors on Hospital Adoption of Technological and Administrative Innovations." *Academy of Management Journal* 24 (1981): 689–713.

Kitchell, Susan. "Corporate Culture, Environmental Adaptation, and Innovation Adoption: A Qualitative/Quantitative Approach." *Journal of the Academy of Marketing Science* 23, no. 3 (1995): 195–205.

Kuhn, Robert Lawrence. "Creative Characters: Entrepreneurs and Chief Executives." In *Handbook for Creative and Innovative Managers,* edited by Robert Lawrence Kuhn, 67–74. New York: McGraw-Hill, 1988.

Kuhn, Robert Lawrence, ed. *Handbook for Creative and Innovative Managers.* New York: McGraw-Hill, 1988.

Kuhn, Robert Lawrence. "What Makes Creative Personality in Business?" In *Handbook for Creative and Innovative Managers,* edited by Robert Lawrence Kuhn, 43–50. New York: McGraw-Hill, 1988.

Kuhn, Robert L., and Raymond Smilor. *Corporate Creativity: Robust Companies and the Entrepreneurial Spirit.* New York: Praeger, 1984.

Lumsden, Charles J. "Evolving Creative Minds: Stories and Mechanisms." In *Handbook of Creativity,* edited by Robert J. Sternberg, 153–168. New York: Cambridge University Press, 1999.

Matathia, Ira, and Marian Salzman. *Next: Trends for the Near Future.* New York: Overlook Press, 1999.

McCauley, Cynthia D., Russ S. Moxley, and Ellen Van Velsor, eds. *The Center for Creative Leadership Handbook of Leadership Development.* San Francisco, CA: Jossey-Bass, 1988.

McClelland, David C. "Characteristics of Successful Entrepreneurs." *Journal of Creative Behavior* 21, no. 3 (1987): 219–233.

Miner, John B. *A Psychological Topography of Successful Entrepreneurs.* Westport, CT: Quorum Books/Greenwood, 1997.

Mumford, Michael D. "Creative Thought: Structure, Components and Educational Implications." *Roeper Review* 21, no. 1 (1998): 14–19.

Panati, Charles. *Panati's Parade of Fads, Foibles, and Manias: The Origins of Our Most Cherished Obsessions.* New York: Harper Collins, 1991.

Perkins, David. "The Topography of Invention." In *Inventive Minds: Creativity in Technology,* edited by Robert John Weber and David N. Perkins, 238–250. New York: Oxford University Press, 1992.

Peters, Tom. *Thriving on Chaos: Handbook for a Management Revolution.* New York: Harper & Row, 1987.

———. *The Circle of Innovation: You Can't Shrink Your Way to Greatness.* New York: Vintage Books, 1999.

Plucker, Jonathan A., and Mark A. Runco. "The Death of Creativity Measurement Has Been Greatly Exaggerated: Current Issues, Recent Advances and Future Directions in Creativity Assessment." *Roeper Review* 21, no. 1 (1998): 36–39.

Ray, Michael, and Rochelle Myers. *Creativity in Business.* New York: Doubleday & Company, 1986.

Runco, Mark A. "Creativity and Its Discontents." In *Creativity and Affect,* edited by Melvin Shaw and Mark Runco, 102–123. Westport, CT: Greenwood, 1994.

Rydz, John S. *Managing Innovation: From the Executive Suite to the Shop Floor.* Cambridge, MA: Ballinger, 1986.

Schrage, Michael. *Serious Play: How the World's Best Companies Simulate to Innovate.* Boston: Harvard Business School Press, 2000.

Scott, Randall K. "Creative Employees: A Challenge to Managers." *Journal of Creative Behavior* 29, no. 1 (1995): 64–71.

Simonton, Dean Keith. "Creativity, Leadership and Chance." In *The Nature of Creativity: Contemporary Psychological Perspectives,* edited by Robert J. Sternberg, 11–38. New York: Cambridge University Press, 1988.

———. *Scientific Genius: A Psychology of Science.* New York: Cambridge University Press, 1988.

Solomon, Daniel, Marilyn Watson, Victor Battistich, and Eric Schaps. "Creating Classrooms That Students Experience as Communities." *American Journal of Community Psychology* 24, no. 6 (1996): 719–748.

Sternberg, Robert J. "The Triarchic Theory of Intelligence." In *Contemporary Assessment: Theories, Tests and Issues,* edited by Dawn Flanagan and Judy Genshaft, 92–104. New York: Guilford Press, 1997.

Stonecipher, Harry C. "Innovation and Creativity: From the Light Bulb to the Jet Engine and Beyond." In *Vital Speeches of the Day.* New York: City News, 1998.

Suarez-Villa, Luis. "Invention, Inventive Learning and Innovation Capacity." *Behavioral Science* 35, no. 4 (1990): 290–312.

Vernon, P. E., ed. *Creativity.* New York: Penguin Books, 1970.

Weber, Robert J., and David N. Perkins, eds. *Inventive Minds: Creativity in Technology.* New York: Oxford University Press, 1992.

Wheatley, Margaret J. *Leadership and the New Science: Learning about Organization from an Orderly Universe.* San Francisco, CA: Berrett-Koehler Publishers, Inc., 1992.

Zander, Rosamund Stone, and Benjamin Zander. *The Art of Possibility: Transforming Professional and Personal Life.* Boston: Harvard Business School Press, 2000.

Jeff Mauzy is a Consulting Manager at Synectics Corporation, an international consulting firm that has been a pioneer in the discovery and application of the principles of creativity and innovation for business. He is also Cofounder and CEO of Inventive Logic, Inc., a company that develops creativity augmenting software. He guest lectures at colleges in the Cambridge, Massachusetts area on personal creativity and team creative problem solving.

Prior to his study of creativity in business, Mauzy was a full-time artist. For three years he was Artist in Residence for the city of Cambridge. He is still a practicing artist, in both painting and large-scale environmental/conceptual work.

Mauzy is the author of "Managing Personal Creativity" in *Innovationforschung und Technologiemanagement.*

Richard Harriman is Managing Partner of Synectics Corporation. He splits his time between firmwide leadership responsibilities, working with clients on specific creativity challenges, and assisting clients in building creativity into their organizations. With Terry Gilliam, a partner at Synectics, he holds a patent for Synectics InSync, a meeting software that supports collaborative resolution to business problems, whether participants are in the same time or place or dispersed.

Harriman has previously held positions in marketing management and new product development at General Foods Corporation. He holds an M.B.A. from Columbia University.

Harriman is the author of chapters in *Handbook for Creative and Innovative Managers* and *New Directions in Creative and Innovative Management: Bridging Theory and Practice.*

We believe that creativity in business, and in particular systemic creativity, is in its adolescent stage of development, with a great deal more to be discovered, codified, and shared. We very much welcome learning about your trials, tribulations, and successes in fostering creativity. Please contact us directly or go to our Web site to find opportunities for dialogue and sharing among those interested in this field.

jmauzy@synectics.com
rharriman@synectics.com
http://www.synecticsworld.com